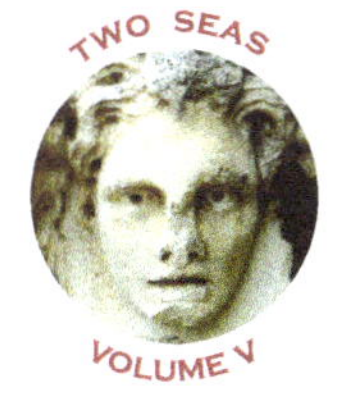

Cold Pizza & Orange Juice

Published by Deuxmers, LLC
PO Box 437305, Kamuela, HI 96743
deuxmers.com

The characters, names, organizations, places and incidents portrayed in this book are either the product of the author's imagination or used fictitiously to convey a sense of realism.

Printed in the United States of America.
ISBN: 978-1-944521-25-7
First edition, January 2026

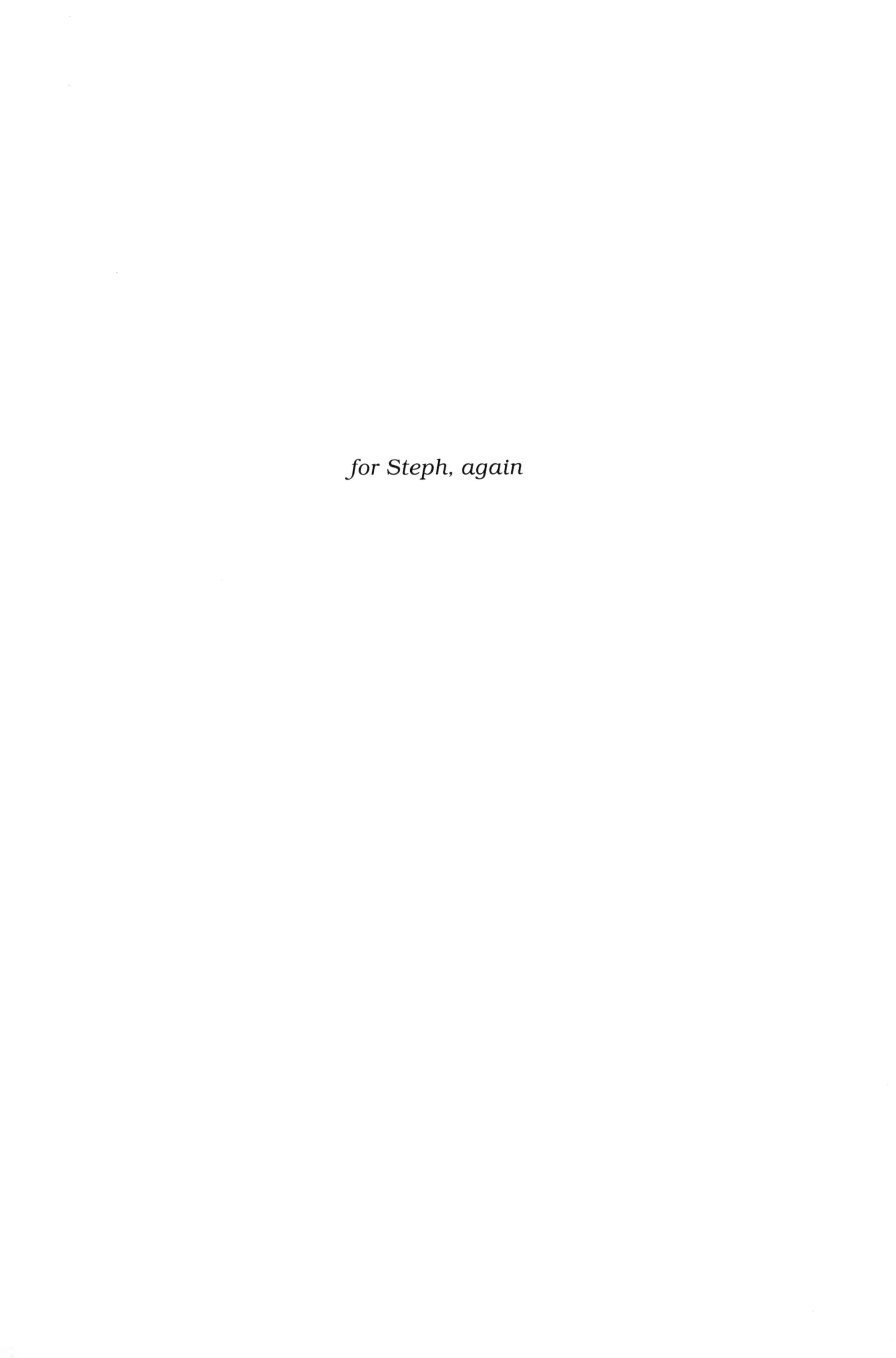

for Steph, again

Cold Pizza & Orange Juice

TONY KILE

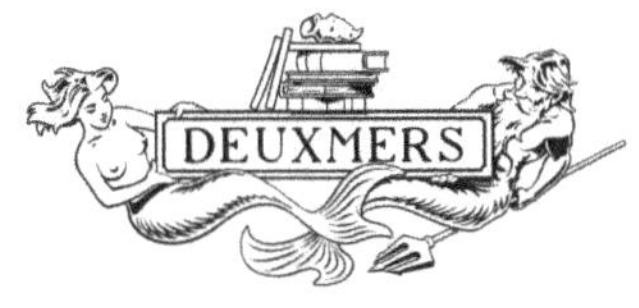

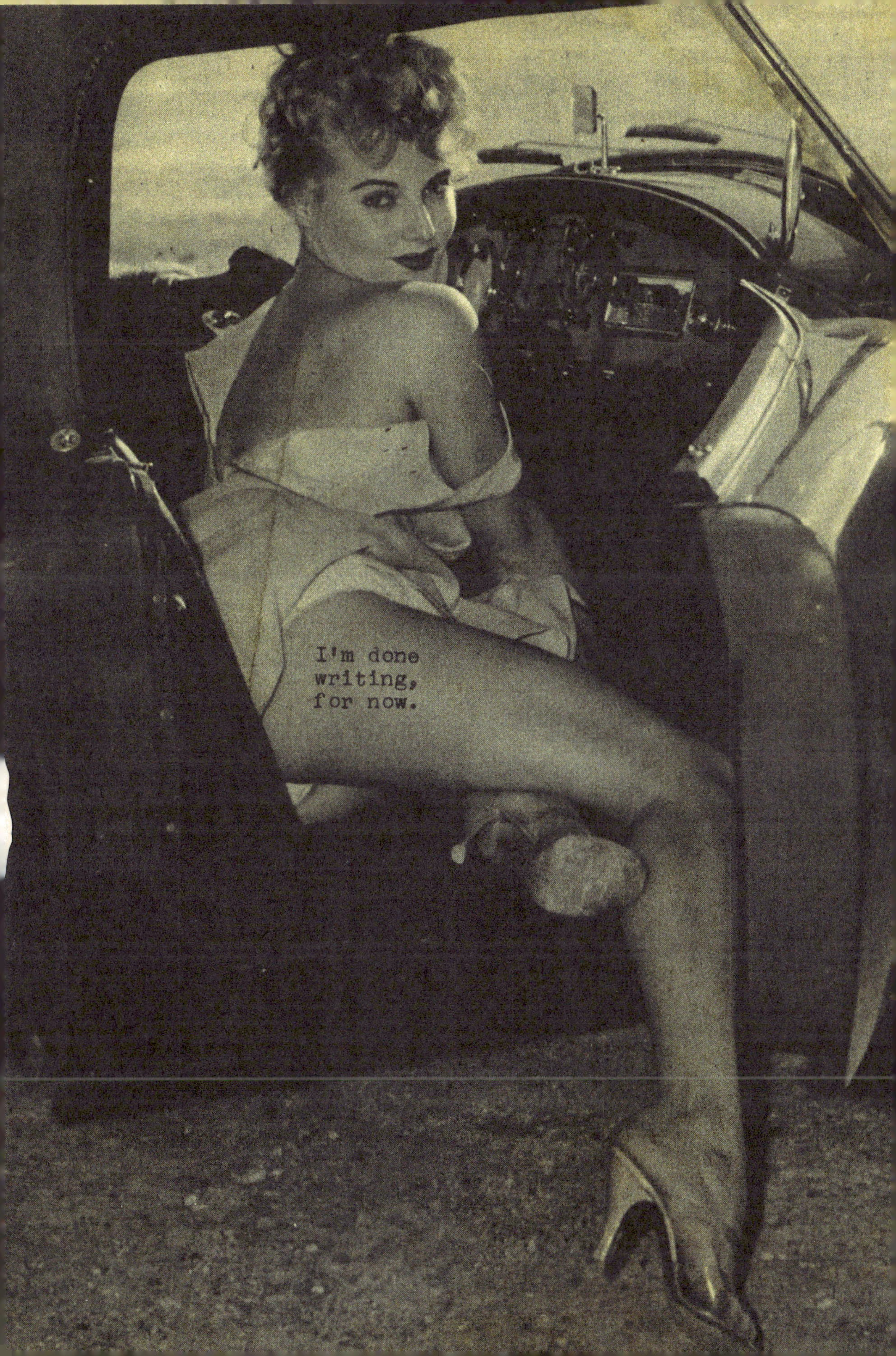
I'm done
writing,
for now.

"i love you tony"

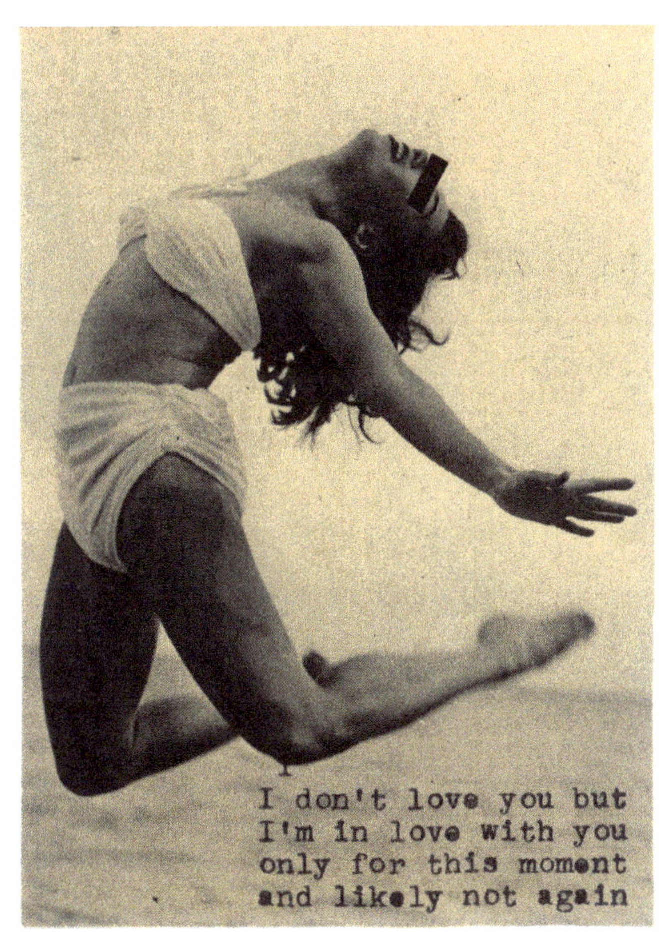
I don't love you but
I'm in love with you
only for this moment
and likely not again

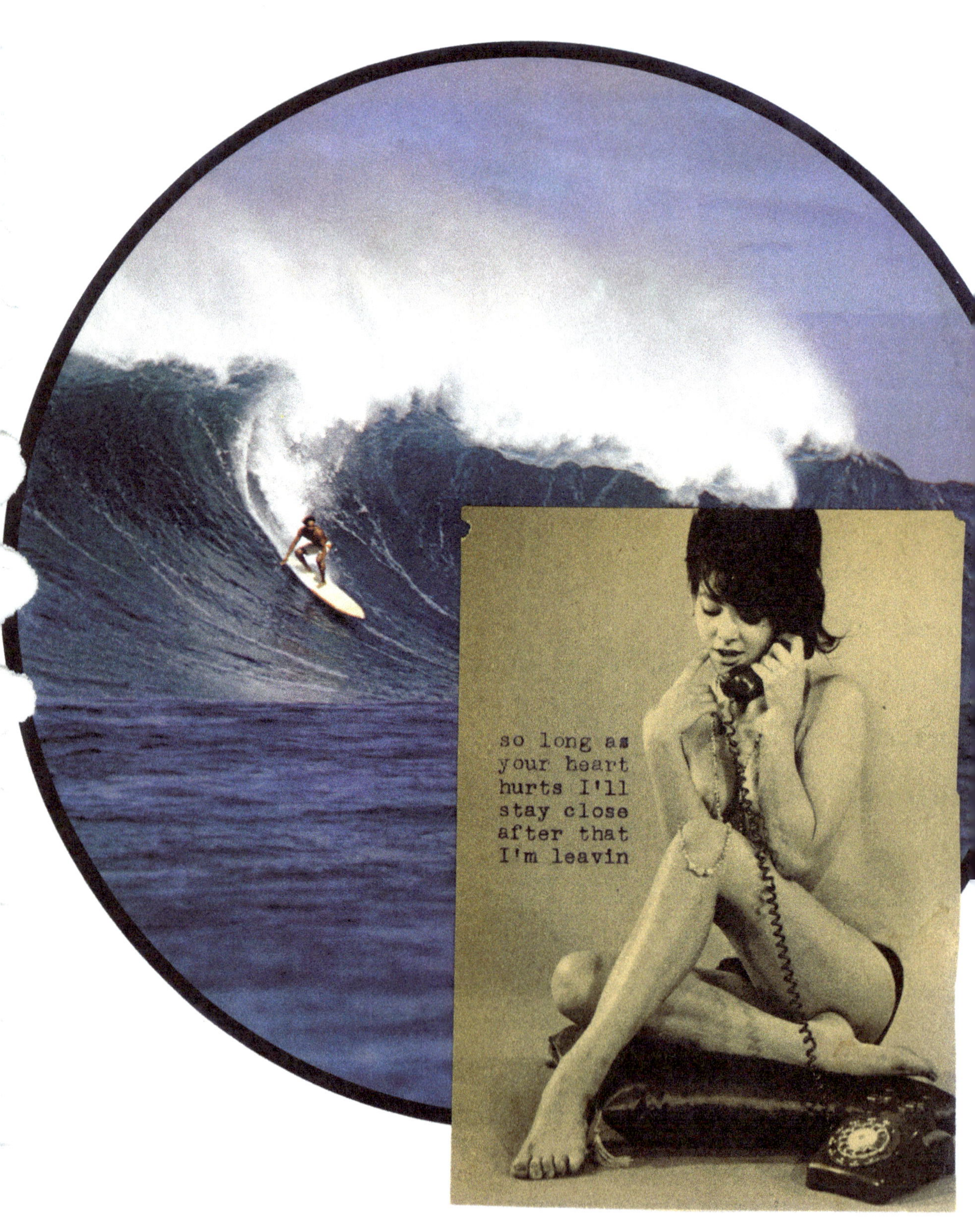
so long as
your heart
hurts I'll
stay close
after that
I'm leavin

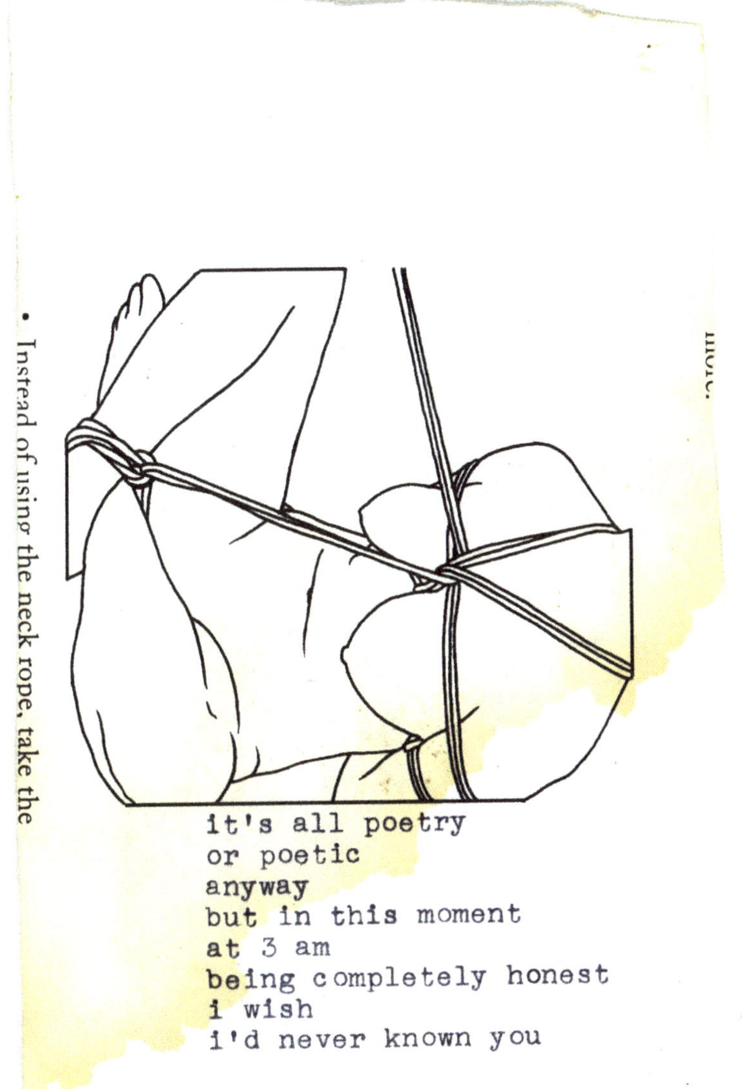

it's all poetry
or poetic
anyway
but in this moment
at 3 am
being completely honest
i wish
i'd never known you

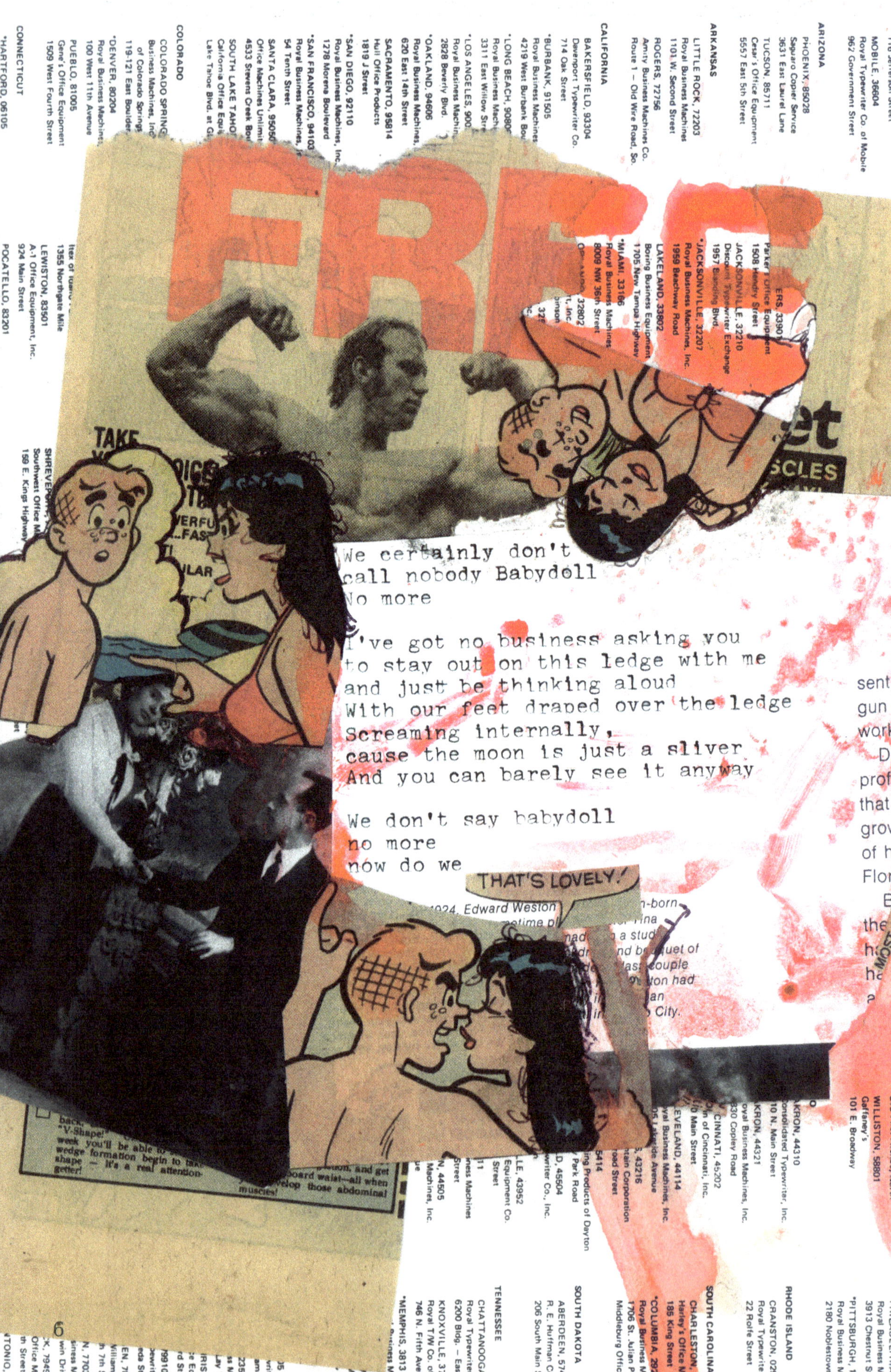
FREE
We certainly don't
call nobody Babydoll
No more

I've got no business asking you
to stay out on this ledge with me
and just be thinking aloud
With our feet draped over the ledge
Screaming internally,
cause the moon is just a sliver
And you can barely see it anyway

We don't say babydoll
no more
now do we
THAT'S LOVELY!

Run

I don't seem to understand
anything you know
or what you say
but I try so hard
anyway
And it's such a great
effort I give
it compromises the way
I live
and too
the way I end up thinking
about you
I project
and hate
everything askew
all of it anew

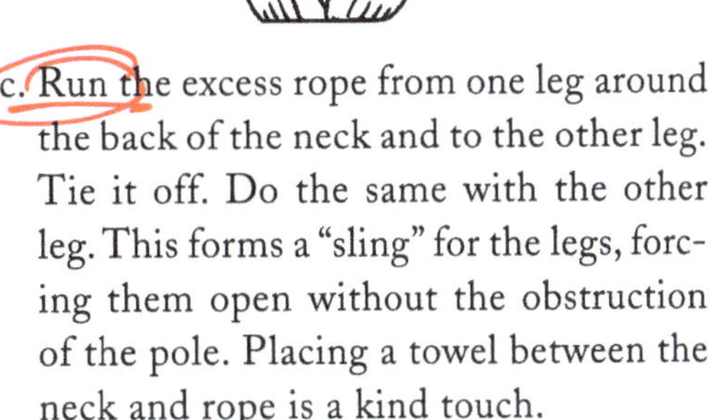

c. Run the excess rope from one leg around the back of the neck and to the other leg. Tie it off. Do the same with the other leg. This forms a "sling" for the legs, forcing them open without the obstruction of the pole. Placing a towel between the neck and rope is a kind touch.

Go and pick some
from the little bitch tree
grab some disappointing apples
while you're too scared to leave
it's unsatisfying shade

Chicken

what else
can be said
about all this
you weren't brave enough
to ever talk about?

Stop crying

what I thought
I knew
about what
I thought
I might ever say
came into question
amidst tears
at two
knowing
you'd probably never
comfort me
here
at two
in tears

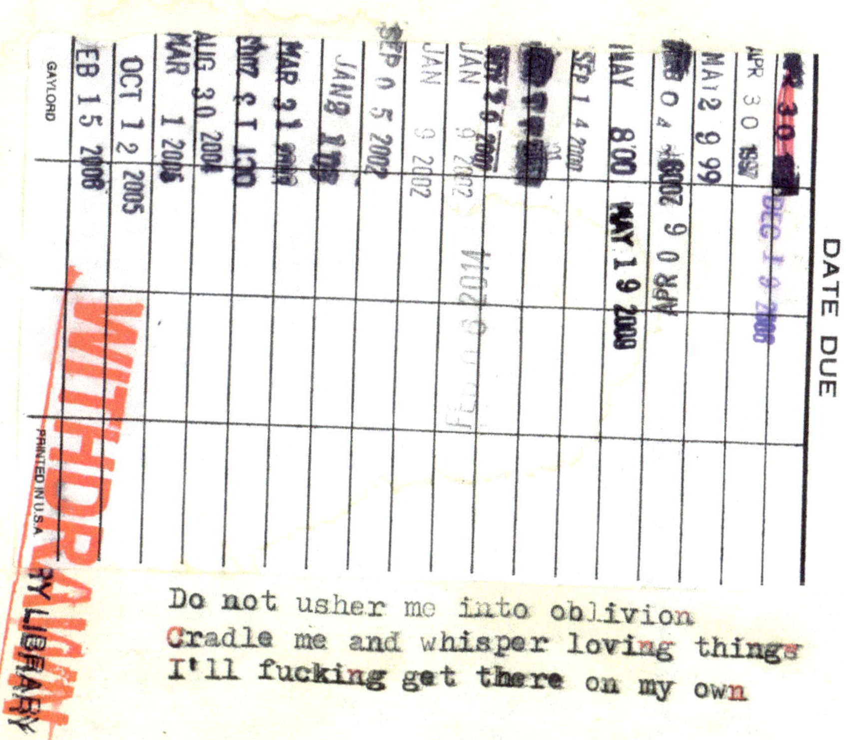

Do not usher me into oblivion
Cradle me and whisper loving things
I'll fucking get there on my own

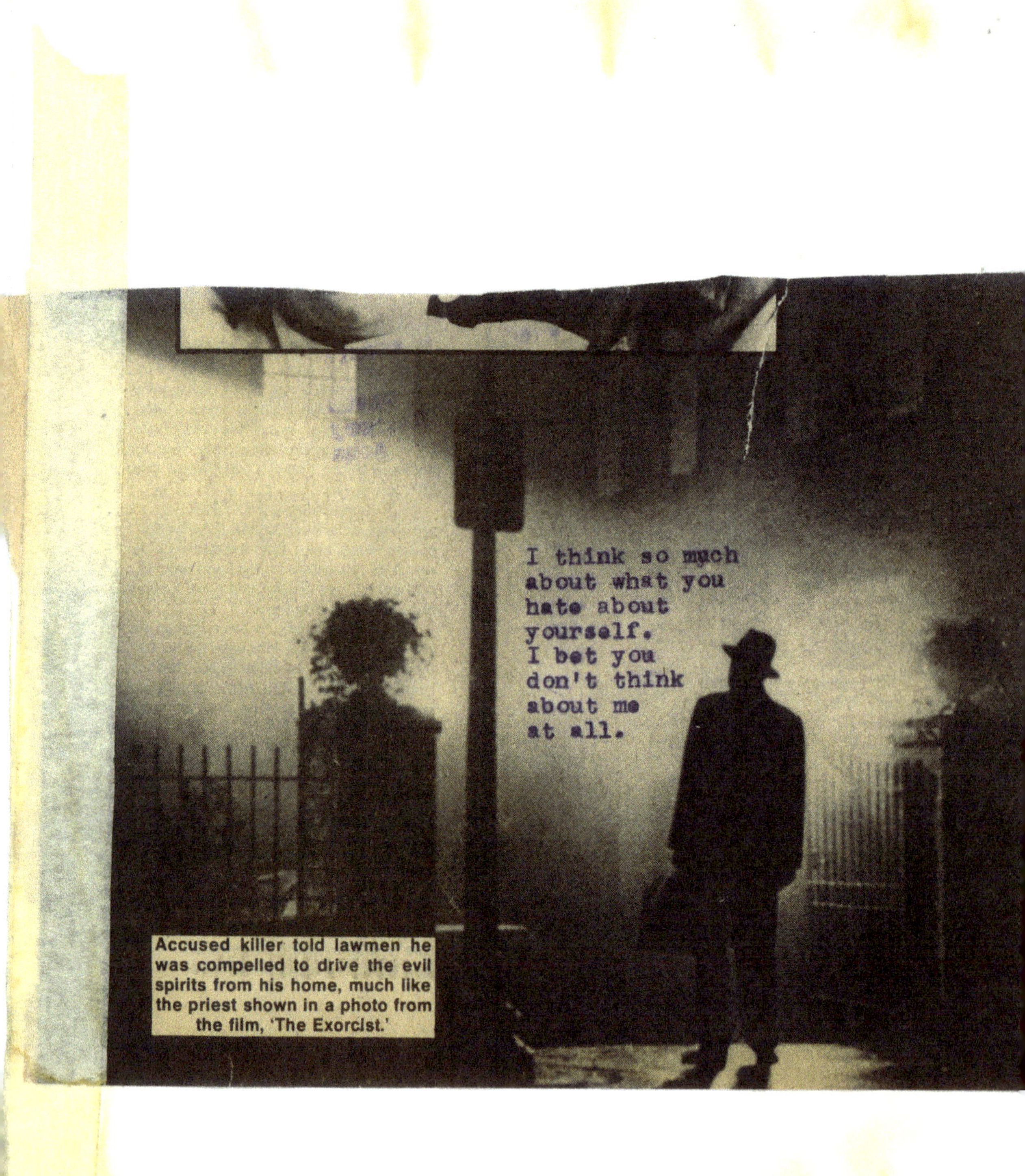
I think so much
about what you
hate about
yourself.
I bet you
don't think
about me
at all.
Accused killer told lawmen he
was compelled to drive the evil
spirits from his home, much like
the priest shown in a photo from
the film, 'The Exorcist.'

Smarter than me

what is it then
that you been ponderin
what's been on your mind?
cause I don't know
but you do know
bout what it is
that's been on mine

"I figured it out!"
I yelled
as I pointed my finger
at my oldest cat.
You gotta figure
how to not want
what it is you feel
you gotta have.
I'm pissin off
whatI've got
and what I want
is playin video games.
how'd I get
so fuckin stupid??
It's something I can
figure out
just maybe
see, I've got
good dick
and a tent

It's true
there are these
fucks
among us
who ain't ever
had to think much
about what thinks a
bout them.
Now then
for the rest of us
fuckin losers
fated
to lose.
One
never-winner
to another
lemme impart some
hard learned knowledge
comes from bein
a loser this long.

It don't matter who cares
it matters who loves you
and nothin has ever loved you
has made you wonder
if they did.

you won't smile if you don't mean it
and you can call that commendable
and true and honest
but they'll just call you a bitch
they don't know maybe
you don't either
if you did smile more.......
you'd just be a smiling bitch

I have to concede
so much honesty
for validation
and you just have to be
and so we will never
know love
together
because
my love
will never
feel
like a need.

you ought not
hate a fool
for being foolish

and I don't hate you

but goddamn
what a fool
you've been

cherish the moments
you're unaware
how much
a fool
you really are

church people are nice

that I'd die soon
so I'll say it now

I was here
for a time
and nobody
really cared
all that much
and then
I wasn't
and really
that's all
I think
anybody should
care
about the whole
affair

I always assumed
that I'd die
soon
so I'll say it now

bold penus
is gud
with star anus

you should go
to church

there's something
hilarious about
my eating
taco bell while
watching the
olympic games
but I'm too
stoned to
say anything
all that funny.

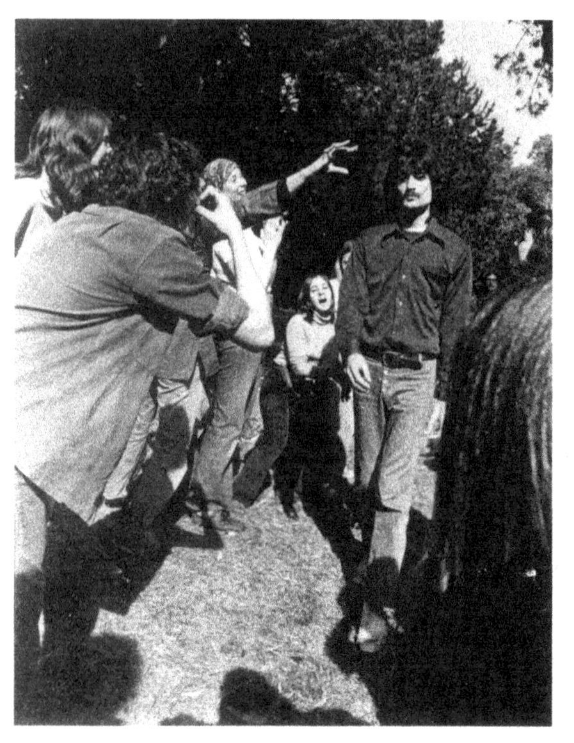

Blind Brunettes

You'd better go lookin
for that moon
'fore you have anything
to say to me.
It's just a sliver
you can barely see
it anyway

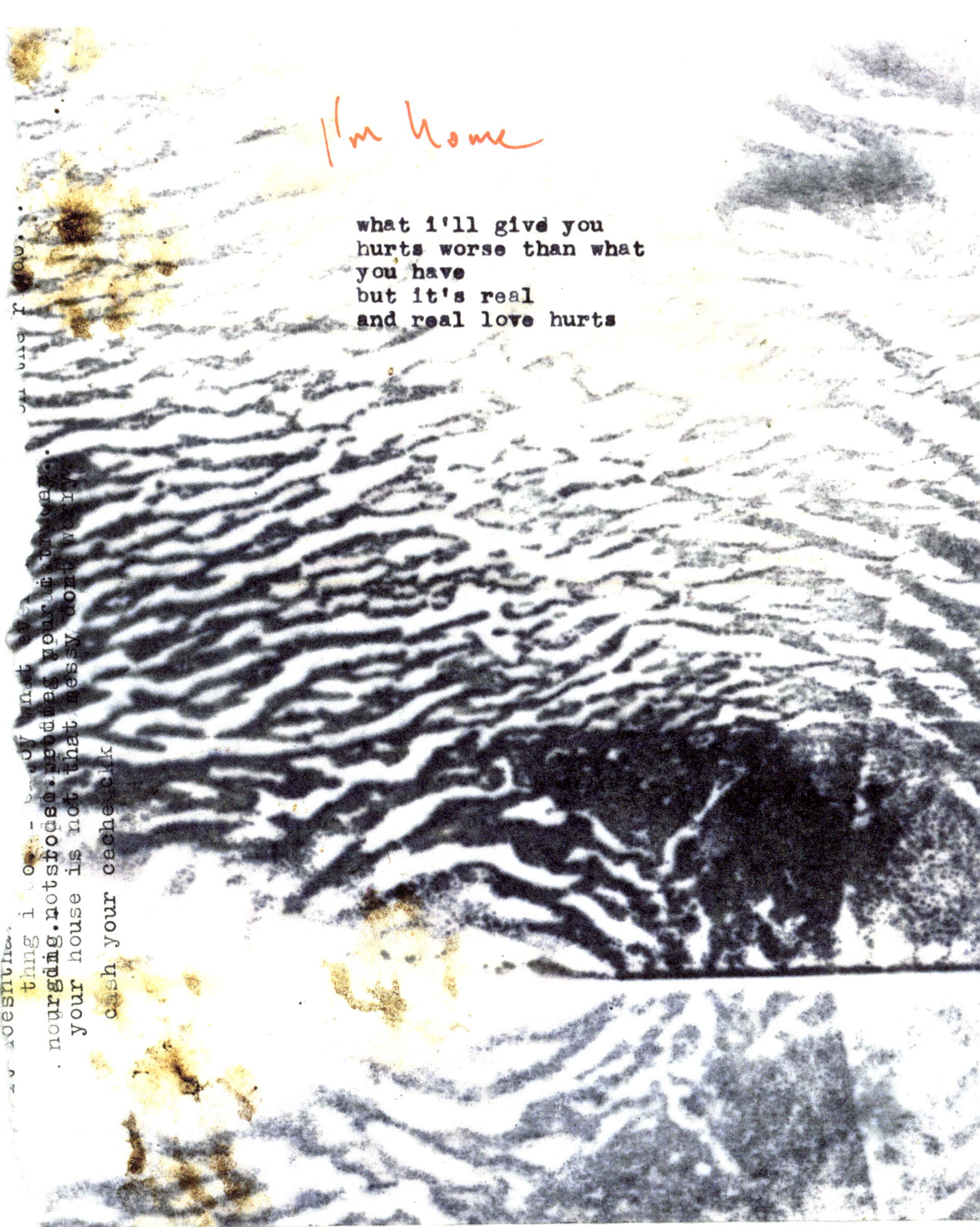
i'm home
what i'll give you
hurts worse than what
you have
but it's real
and real love hurts

Ghosts are real I guess
they just never talk to me
I must not be that interesting
to dead people
they're always fuckin around
with some idiot
but they don't pester me
fuck 'em then
glad they're dead
I'm not cool enough
to haunt

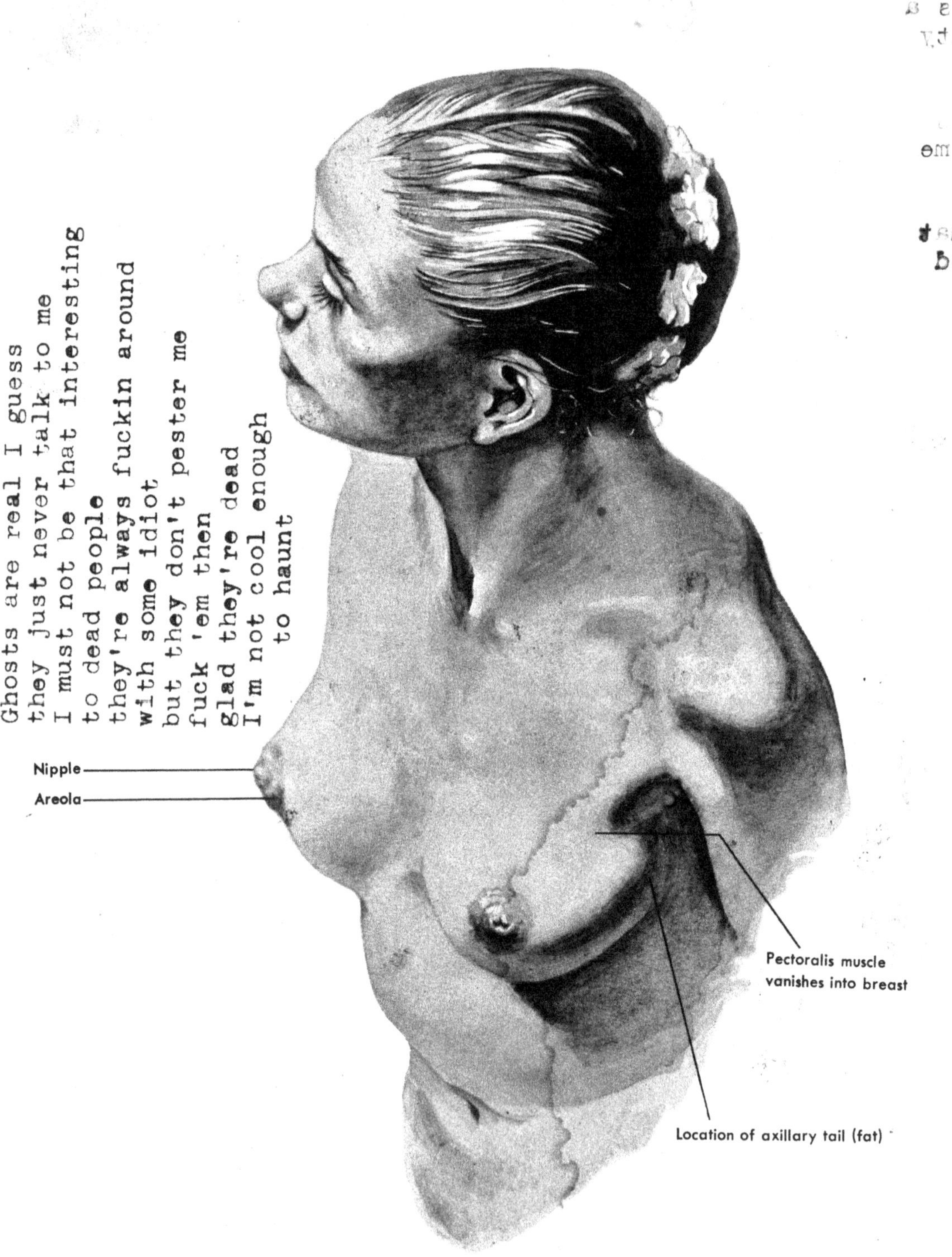

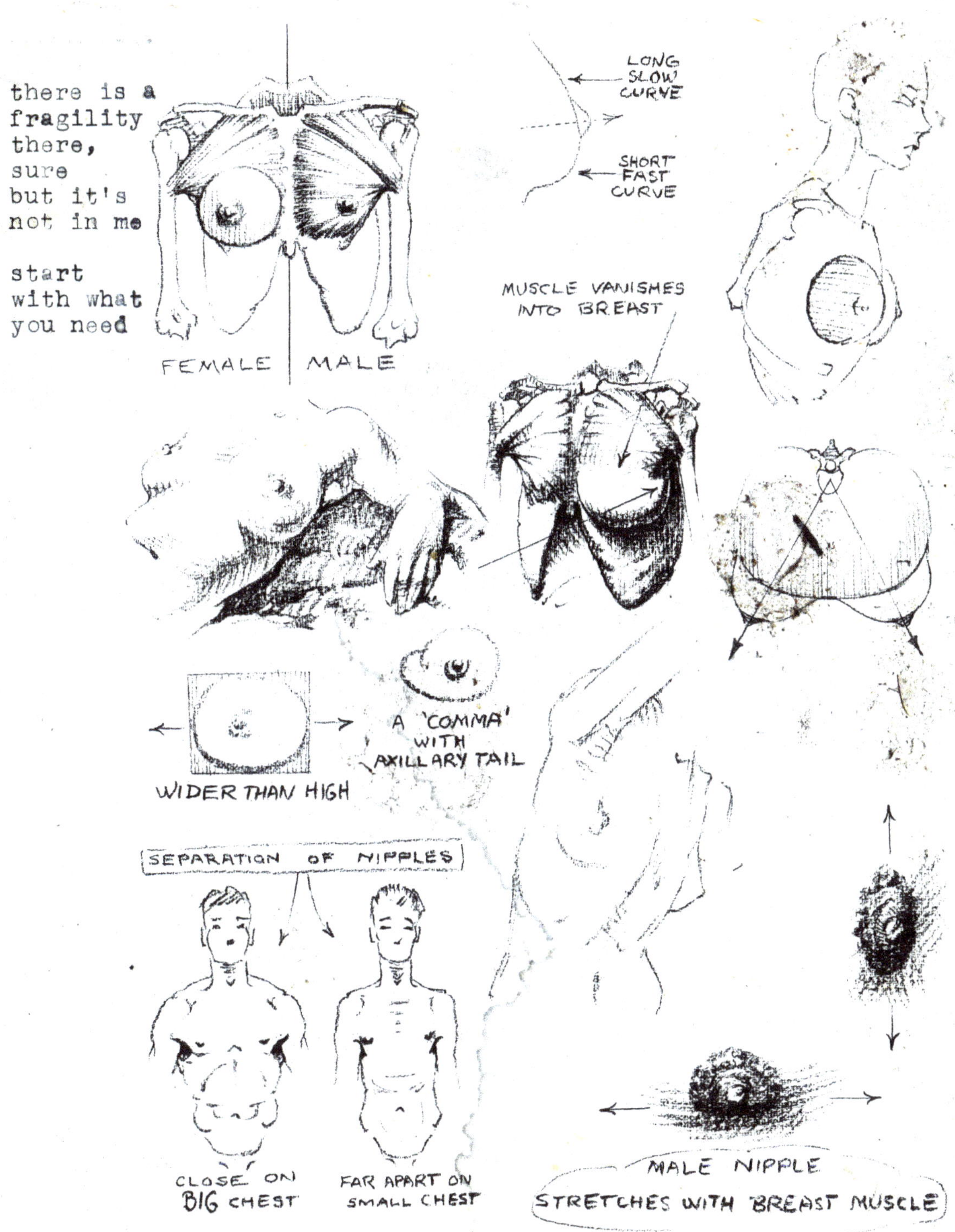
there is a
fragility
there,
sure
but it's
not in me

start
with what
you need
FEMALE
MALE
LONG SLOW CURVE
SHORT FAST CURVE
MUSCLE VANISHES INTO BREAST
WIDER THAN HIGH
A 'COMMA' WITH AXILLARY TAIL
SEPARATION OF NIPPLES
CLOSE ON BIG CHEST
FAR APART ON SMALL CHEST
MALE NIPPLE
STRETCHES WITH BREAST MUSCLE

134 CHAPTER 4 *The Anatomical Factor*

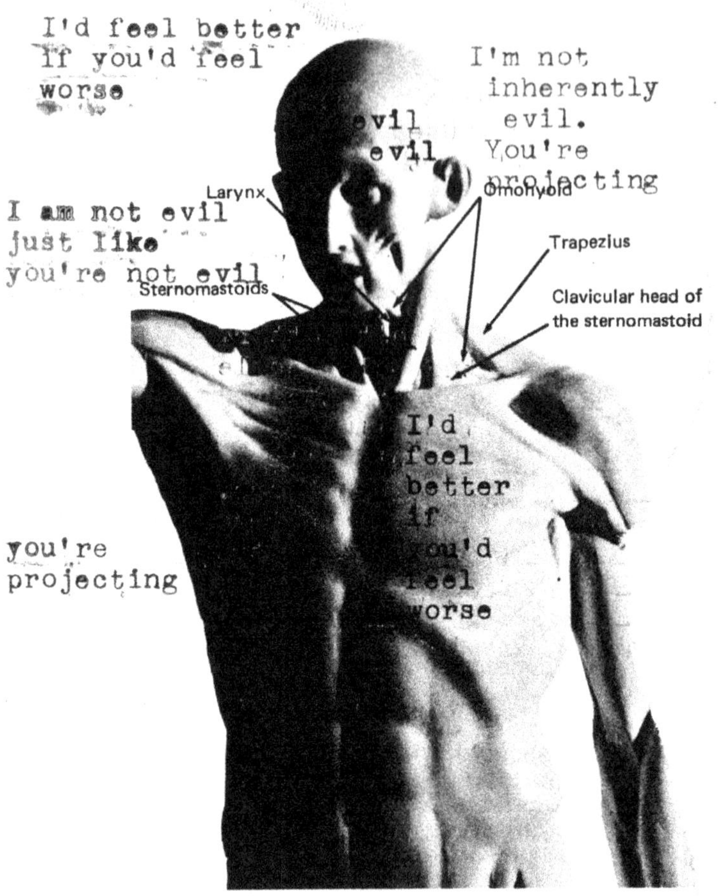

4.14

4.15

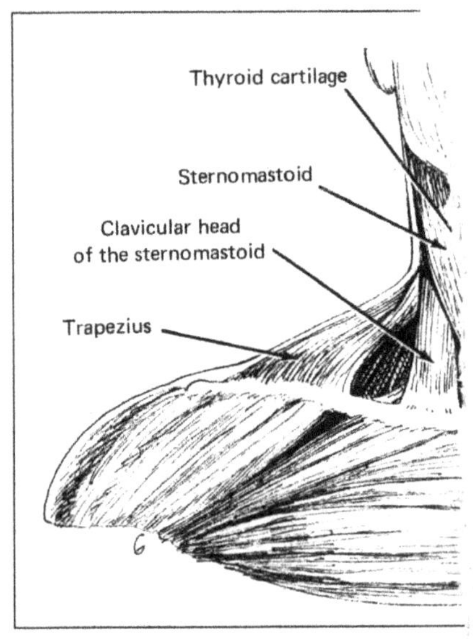

I'd feel better
if you'd feel
worse

I'm not evil
just like
you're not evil
just projecting

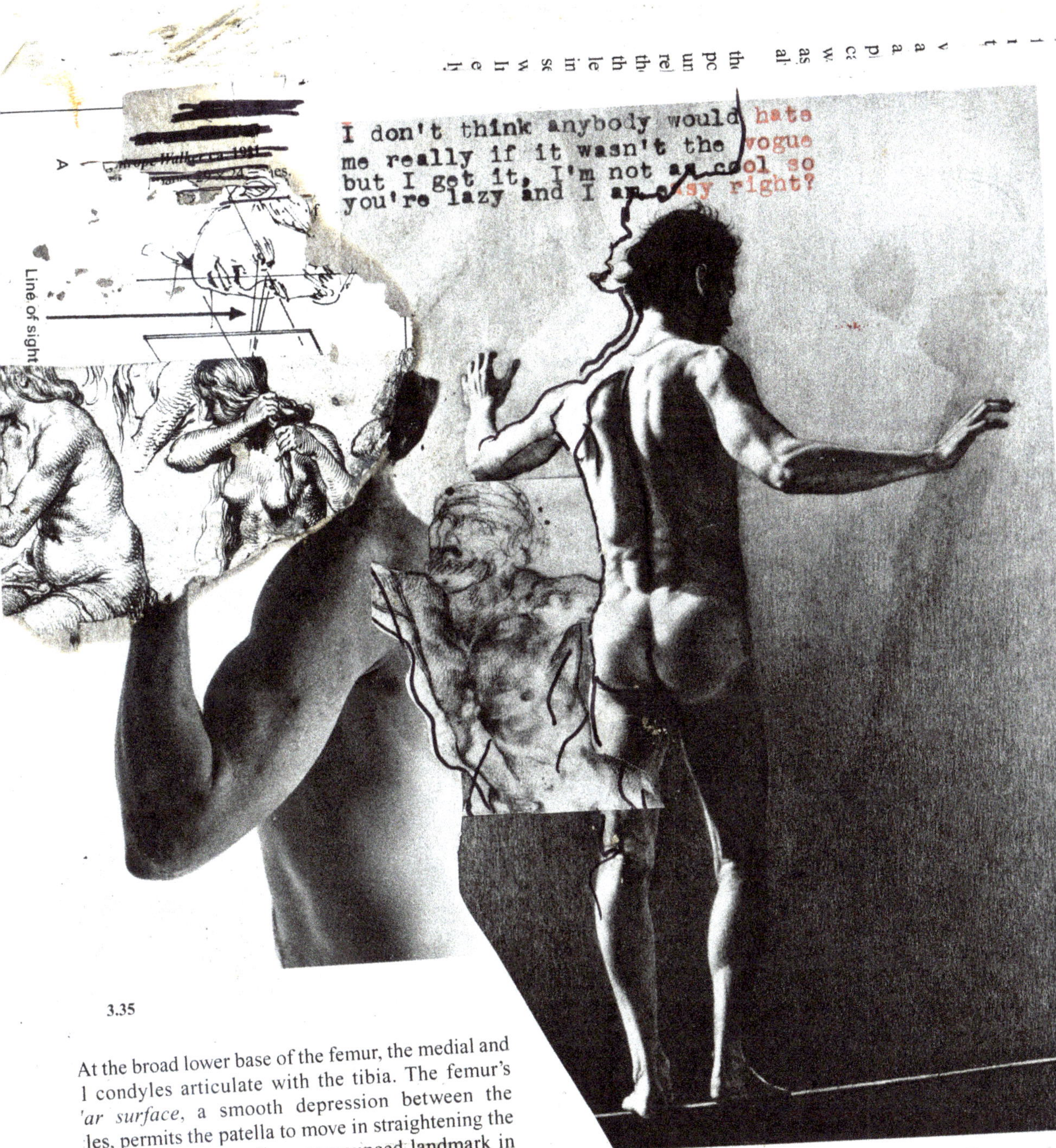
I don't think anybody would hate
me really if it wasn't the vogue
but I get it, I'm not as cool so
you're lazy and I am easy right?
Line of sight
3.35
At the broad lower base of the femur, the medial and
l condyles articulate with the tibia. The femur's
'ar surface, a smooth depression between the
les, permits the patella to move in straightening the
he patella is generally a pronounced landmark in
aightened leg, often protruding at the knee even in

Your choice not mine

I fold pizza
boxes
and think about
how you've only ever
called me a friend
you call me
a friend
you call out
"friend"
though
we both know
you ain't
been much
a friend
to me
but i stopped
foldin pizza
boxes

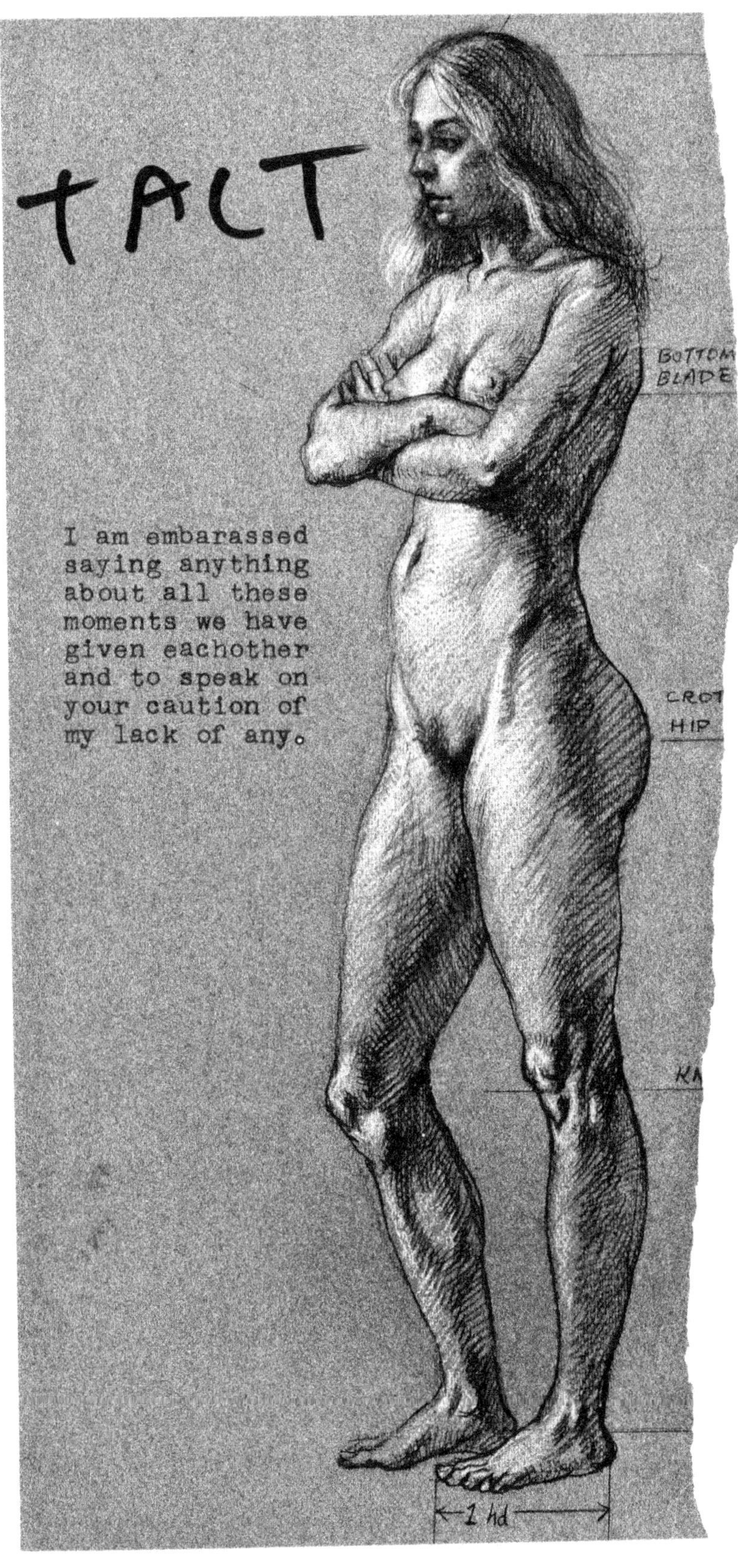

Standing, side view.

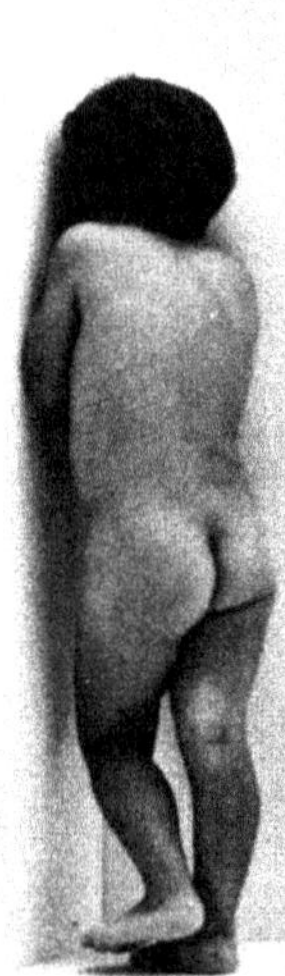

I never made you
think too much
bout one or zero
black or white
with or without
and never forced you
to take any count.
It's not really possible
to know
the exact amount
of whales there are
and I suppose that's why we don't

TAKUYA TSUKAHARA: *White Play*, 1971

Nendo Sho (Annual Award)—Japan

To the photographer, the sterile space he had created in his studio was meant to suggest the barrenness of the modern world. For his four-year-old models, however, it was an ideal playroom. Their spontaneous antics, photographed through a peephole, resulted in a surreal scene of childish fun and games.

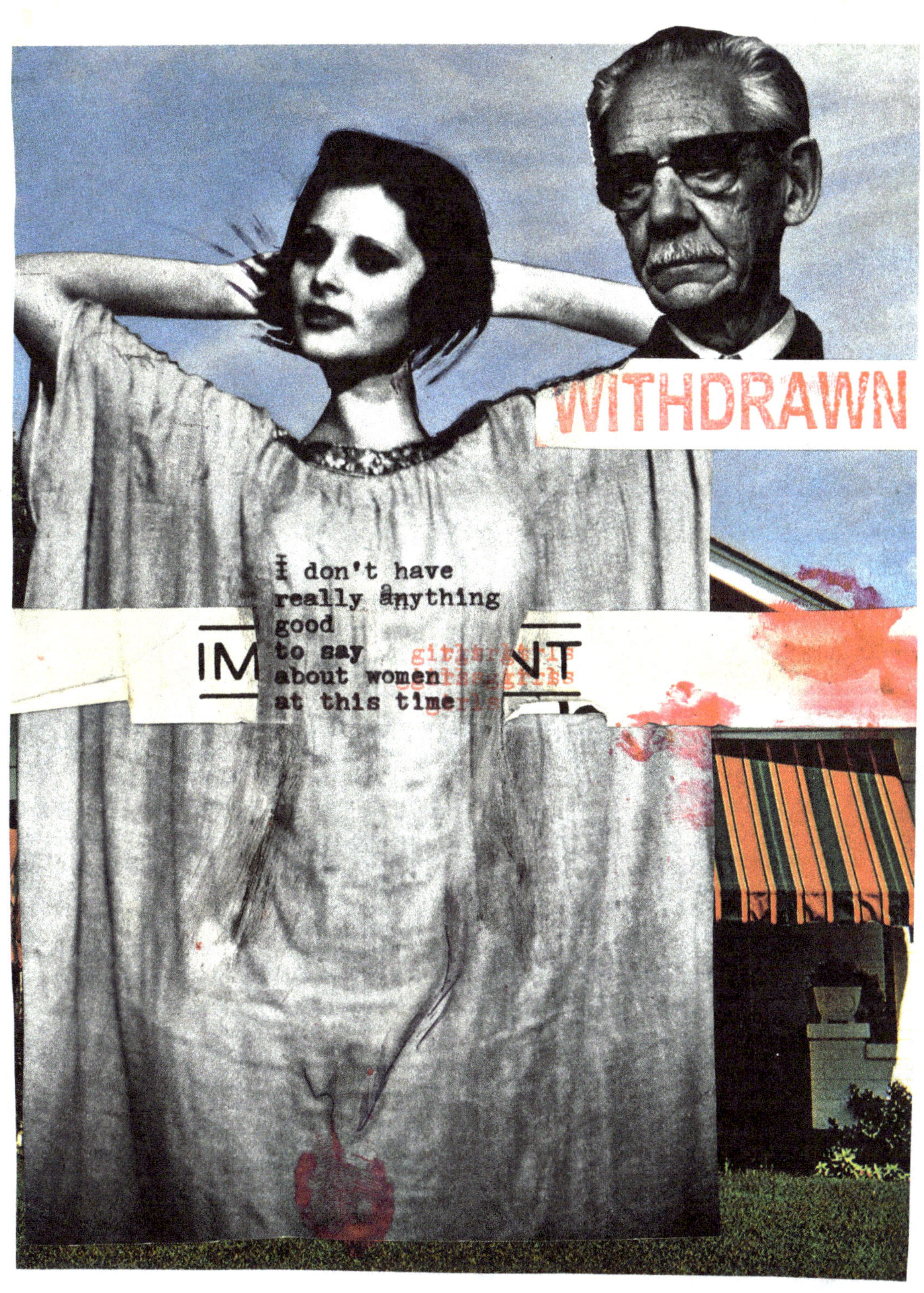
WITHDRAWN
I don't have
really anything
good
to say
about women
at this time
IM
NT

attack + Defense

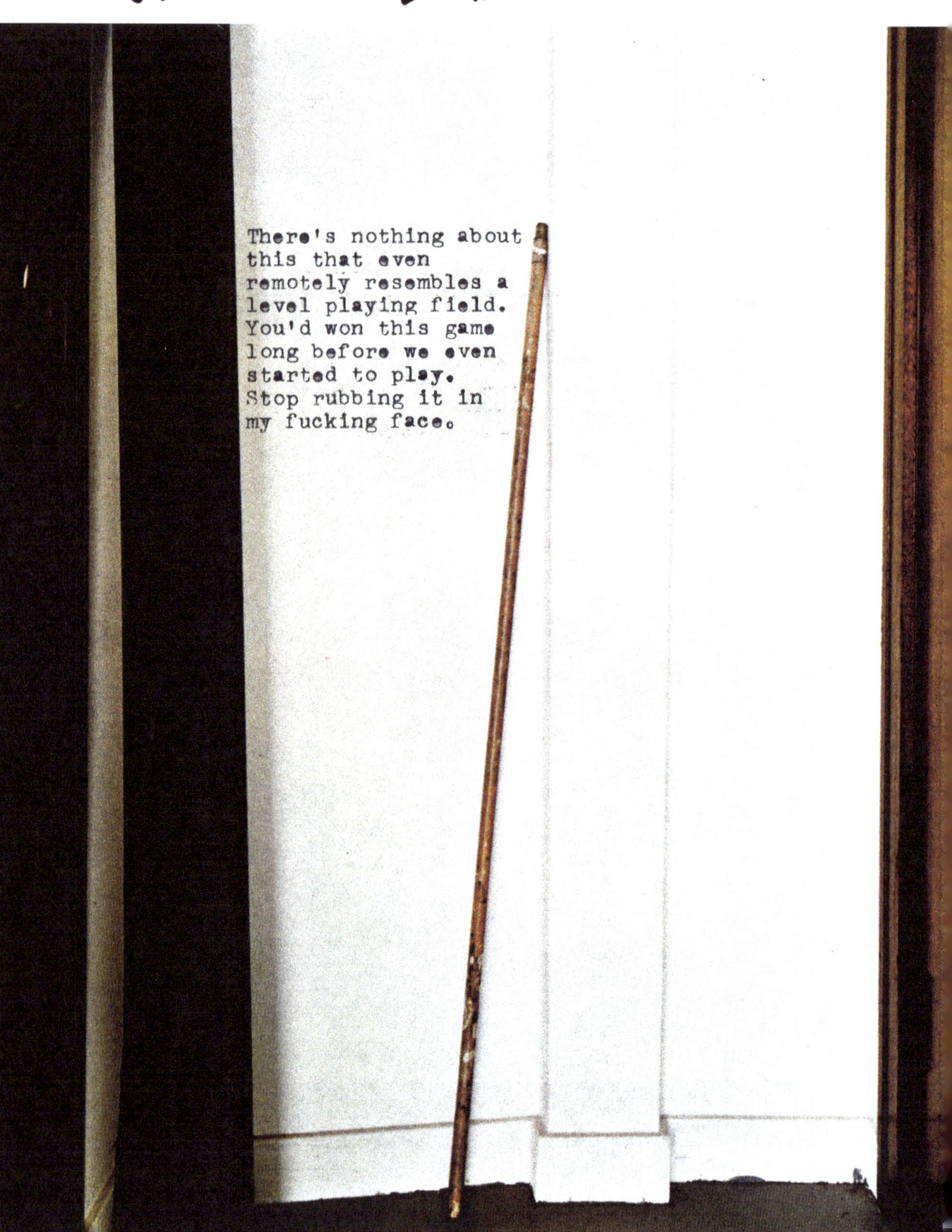

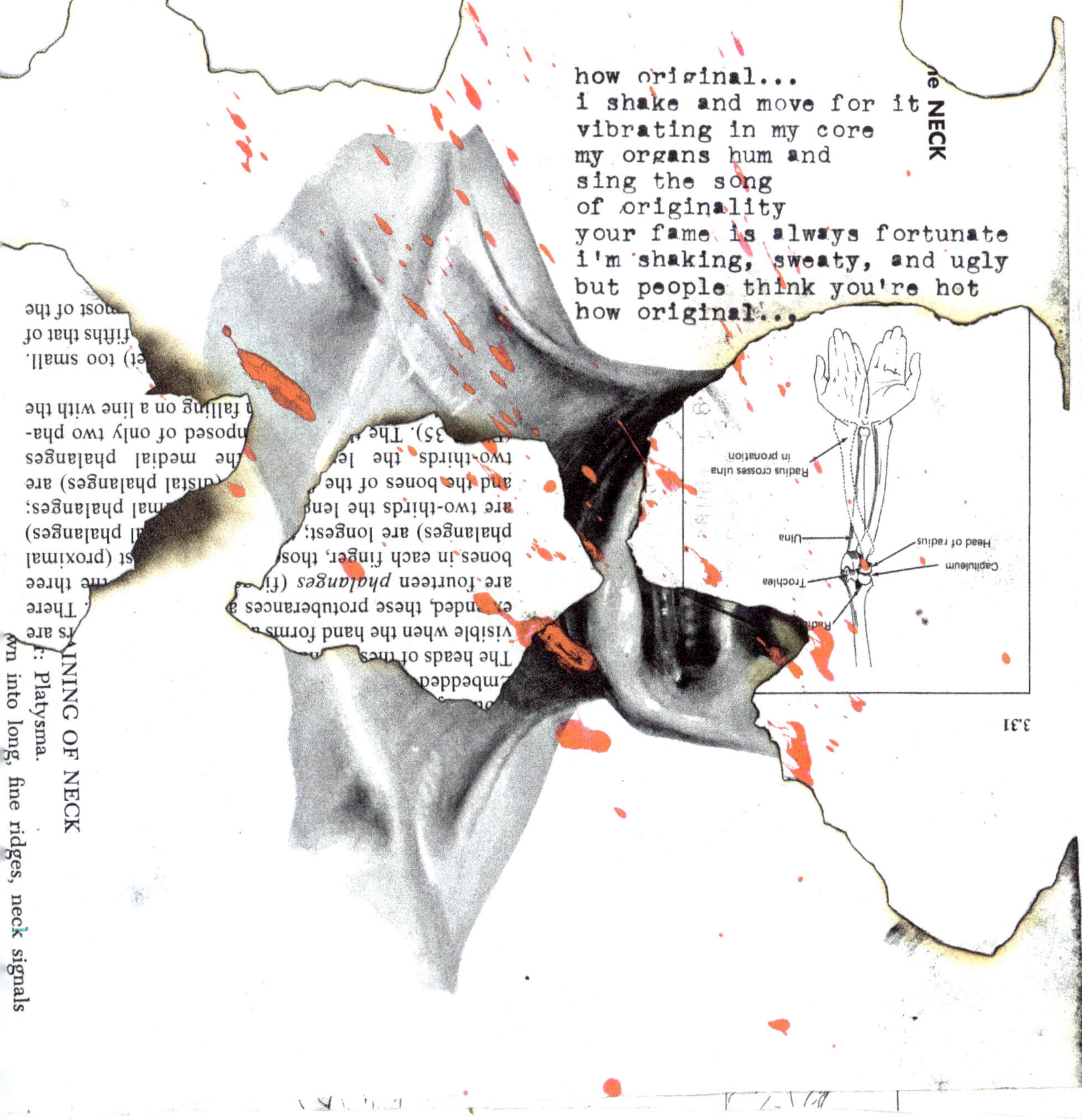
how original...
i shake and move for it
vibrating in my core
my organs hum and
sing the song
of originality
your fame is always fortunate
i'm shaking, sweaty, and ugly
but people think you're hot
how original...

Discover Camel Lights satisfaction.

your pussy ain't
that rock n roll
shit ya think it
is im just sayin

The Camel World of satisfacti
comes to low tar smoki

This is where it all started. Camel qu
now in a rich tasting Camel blend for sm
low tar smoking. Camel Lights brings
solution to taste in low

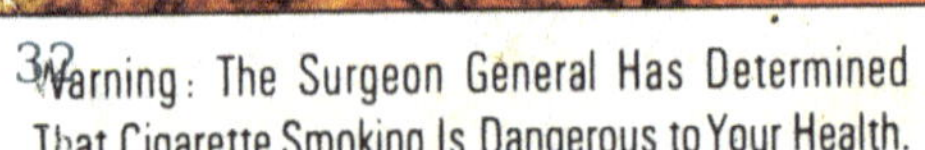

LIGHTS: 10 mg. "tar", 0.8 mg. nicotine, LIGHTS 100's:
13 mg. "tar", 1.0 mg. nicotine, av. per cigarette by FTC

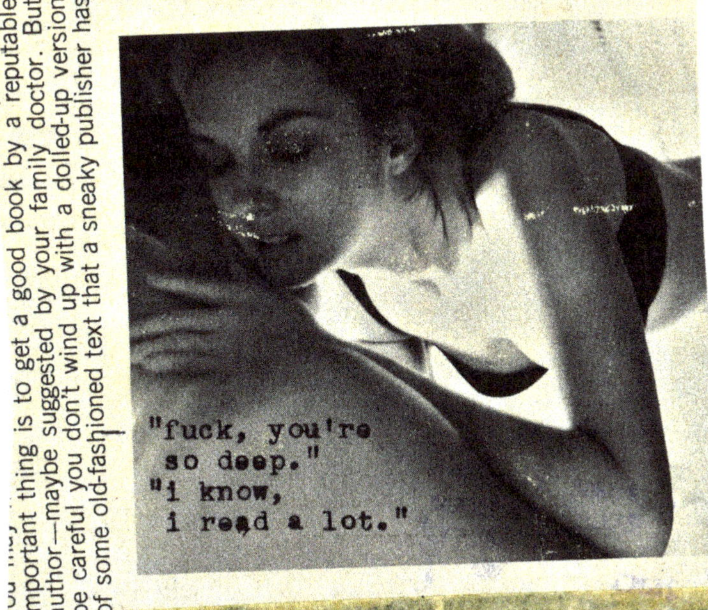
important thing is to get a good book by a reputable
author—maybe suggested by your family doctor. But
be careful you don't wind up with a dolled-up version
of some old-fashioned text that a sneaky publisher has
"fuck, you're
so deep."
"i know,
i read a lot."

your scent and sweat
tastes like being alive

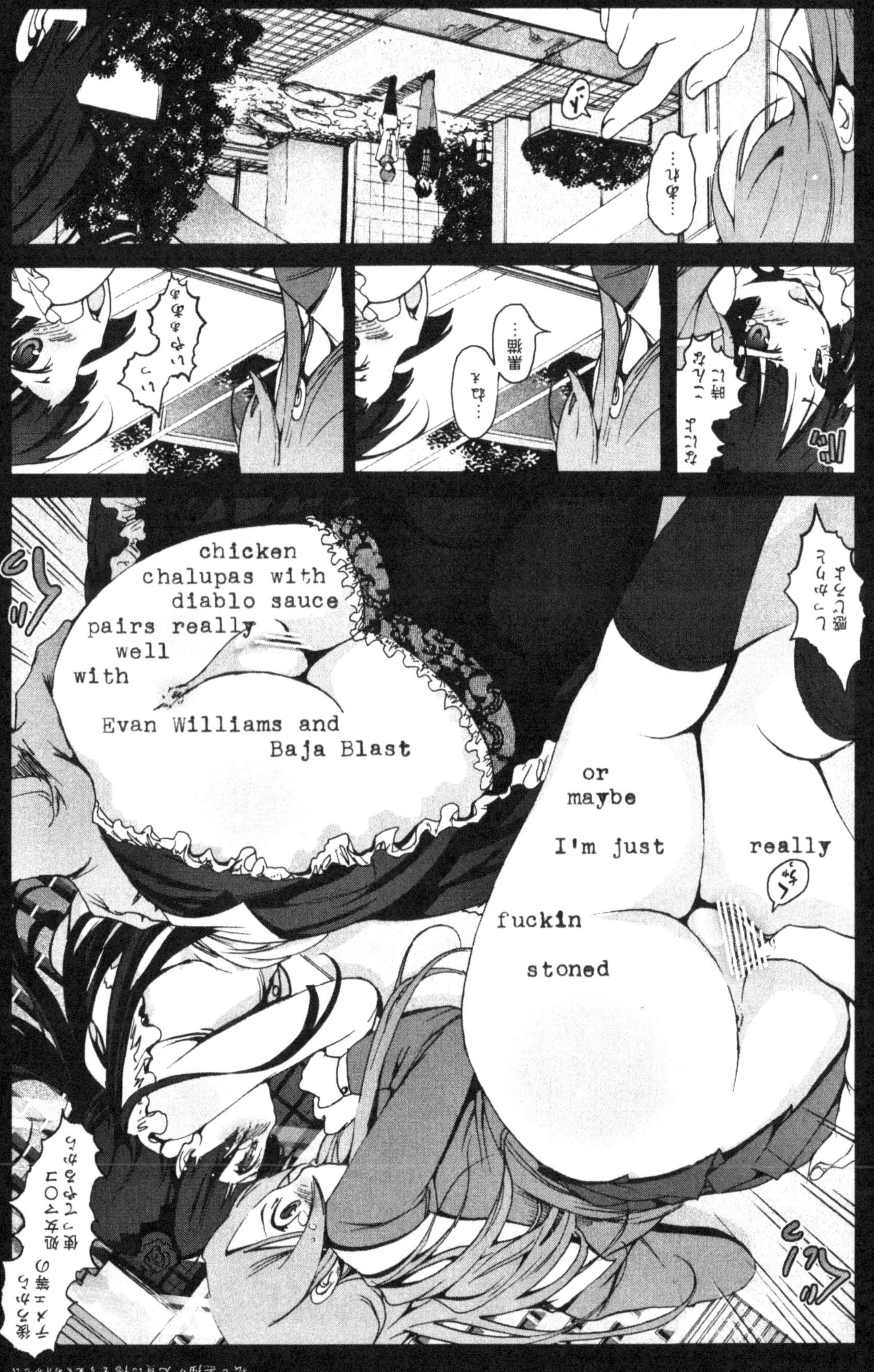
chicken chalupas with diablo sauce pairs really well with
Evan Williams and Baja Blast
or maybe I'm just really fuckin stoned

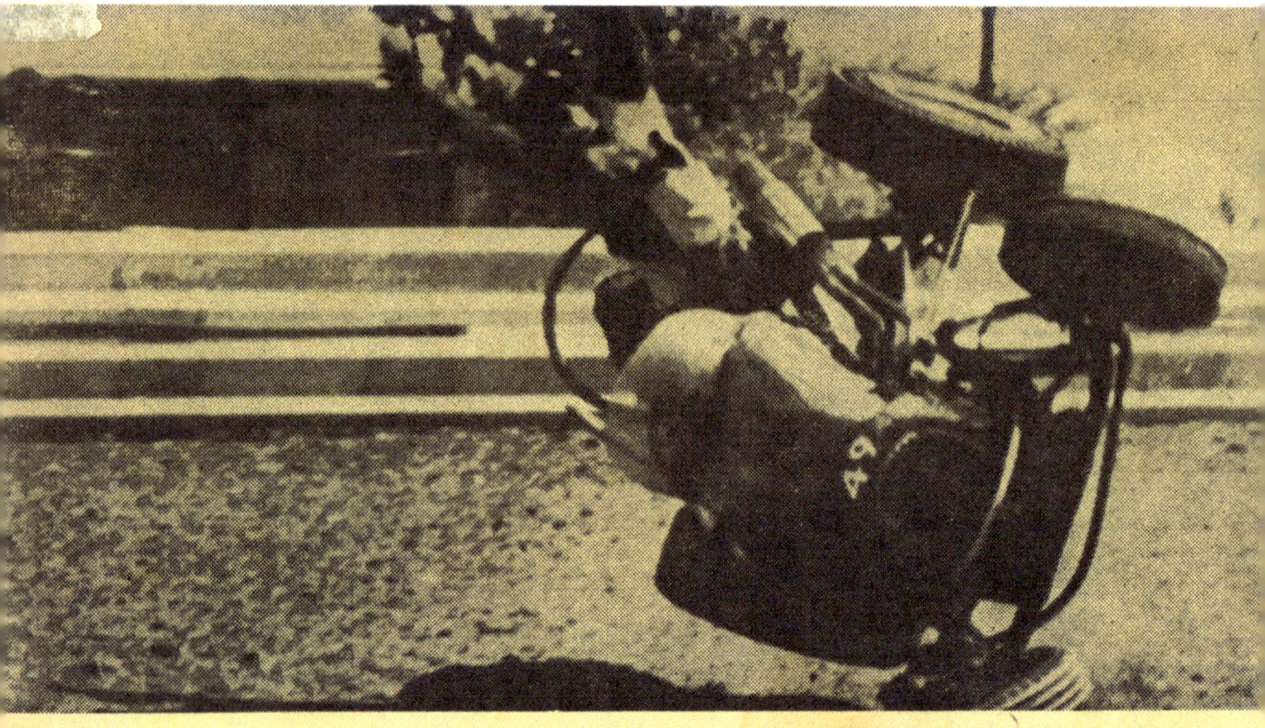

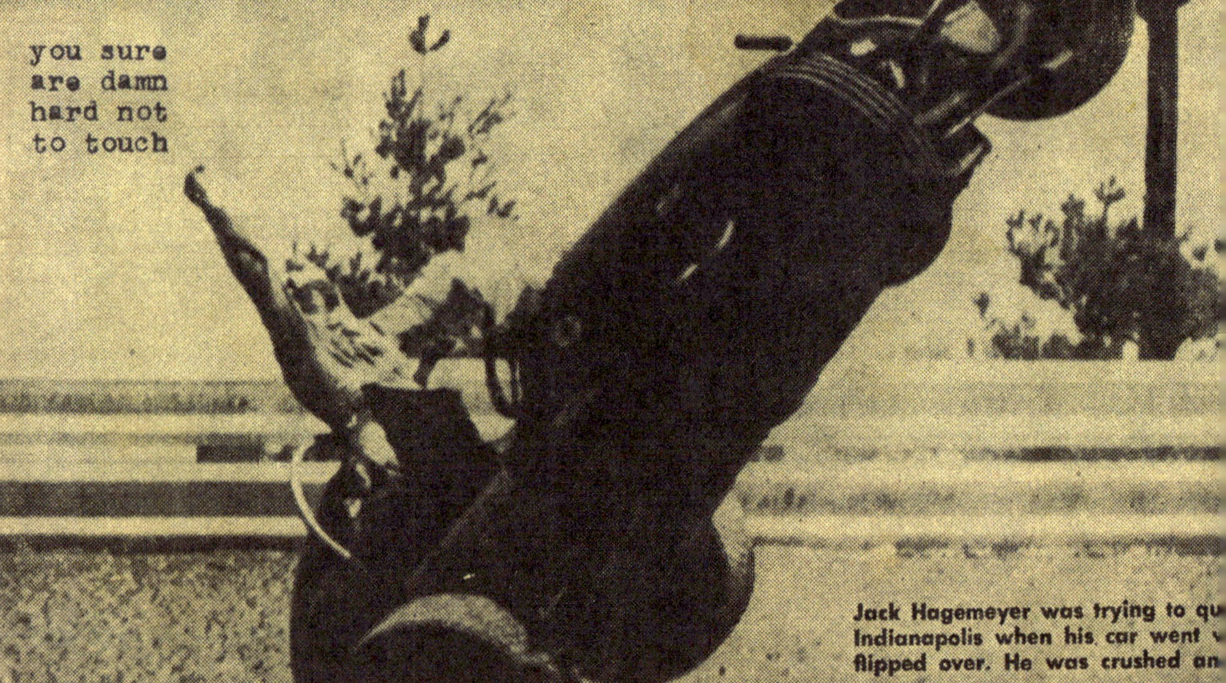

Jack Hagemeyer was trying to qu
Indianapolis when his car went
flipped over. He was crushed an

AUTO RACING

tastes good

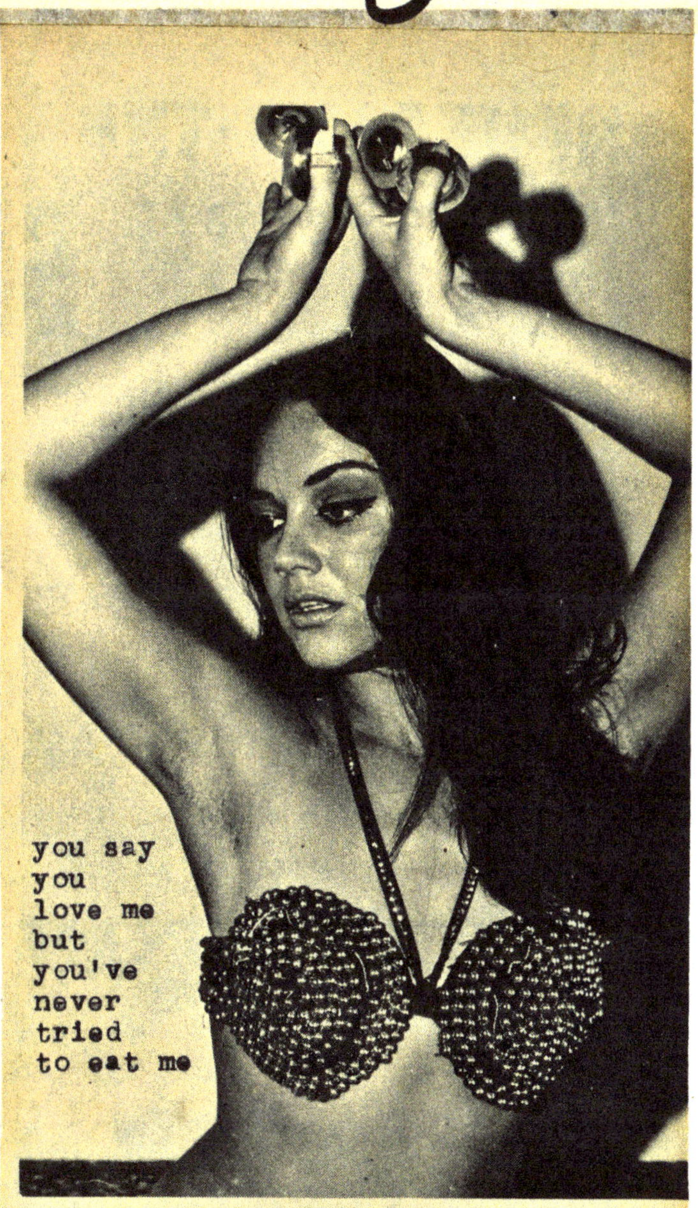

Cat Goddess was most beautiful Egyptian woman who'd ever lived. This girl bears resemblance to sculptured face in tomb.

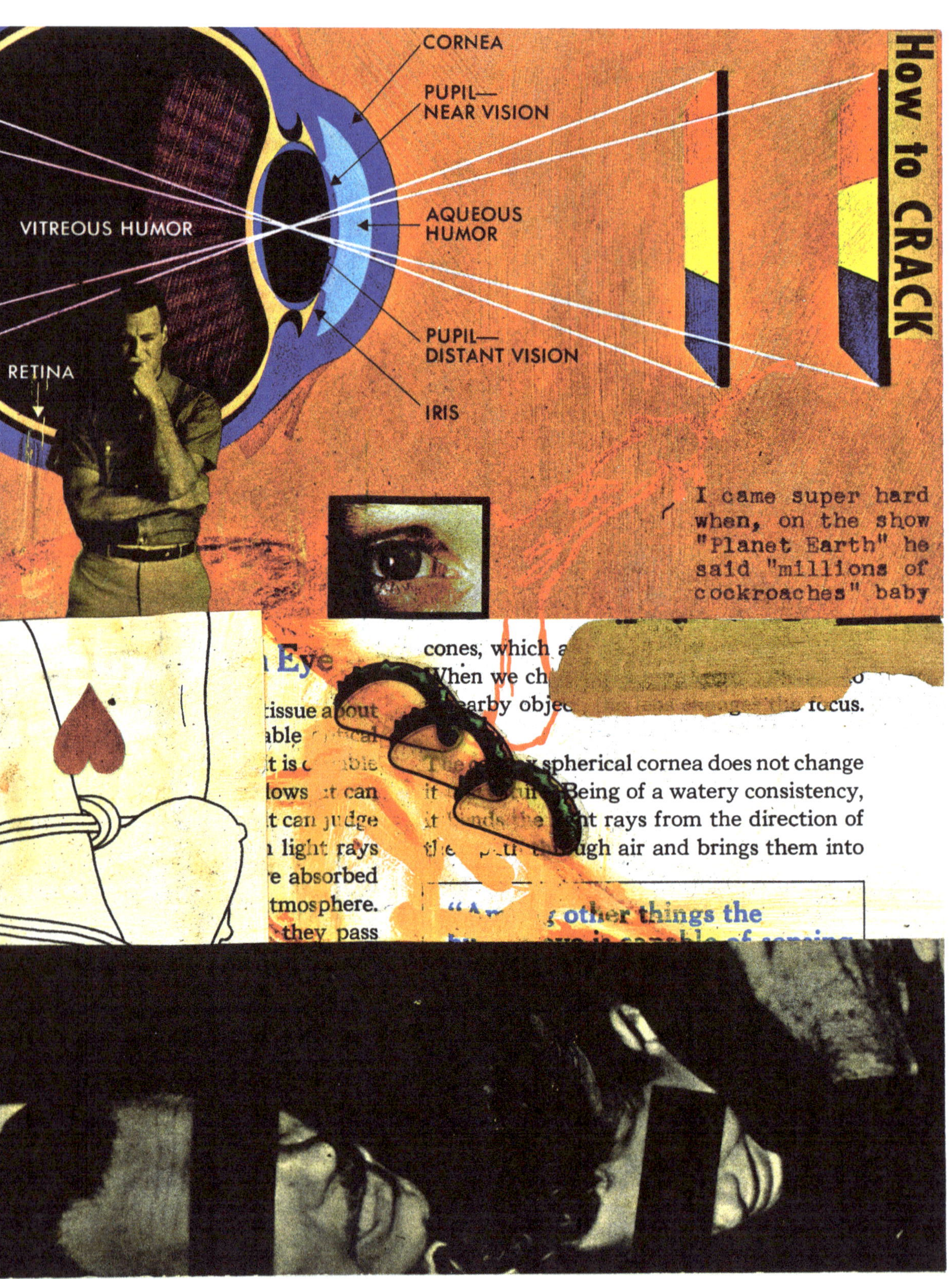
CORNEA
PUPIL—
NEAR VISION
VITREOUS HUMOR
AQUEOUS
HUMOR
PUPIL—
DISTANT VISION
RETINA
IRIS
How to CRACK
I came super hard
when, on the show
"Planet Earth" he
said "millions of
cockroaches" baby
spherical cornea does not change
Being of a watery consistency,
rays from the direction of
air and brings them into
e absorbed
tmosphere.

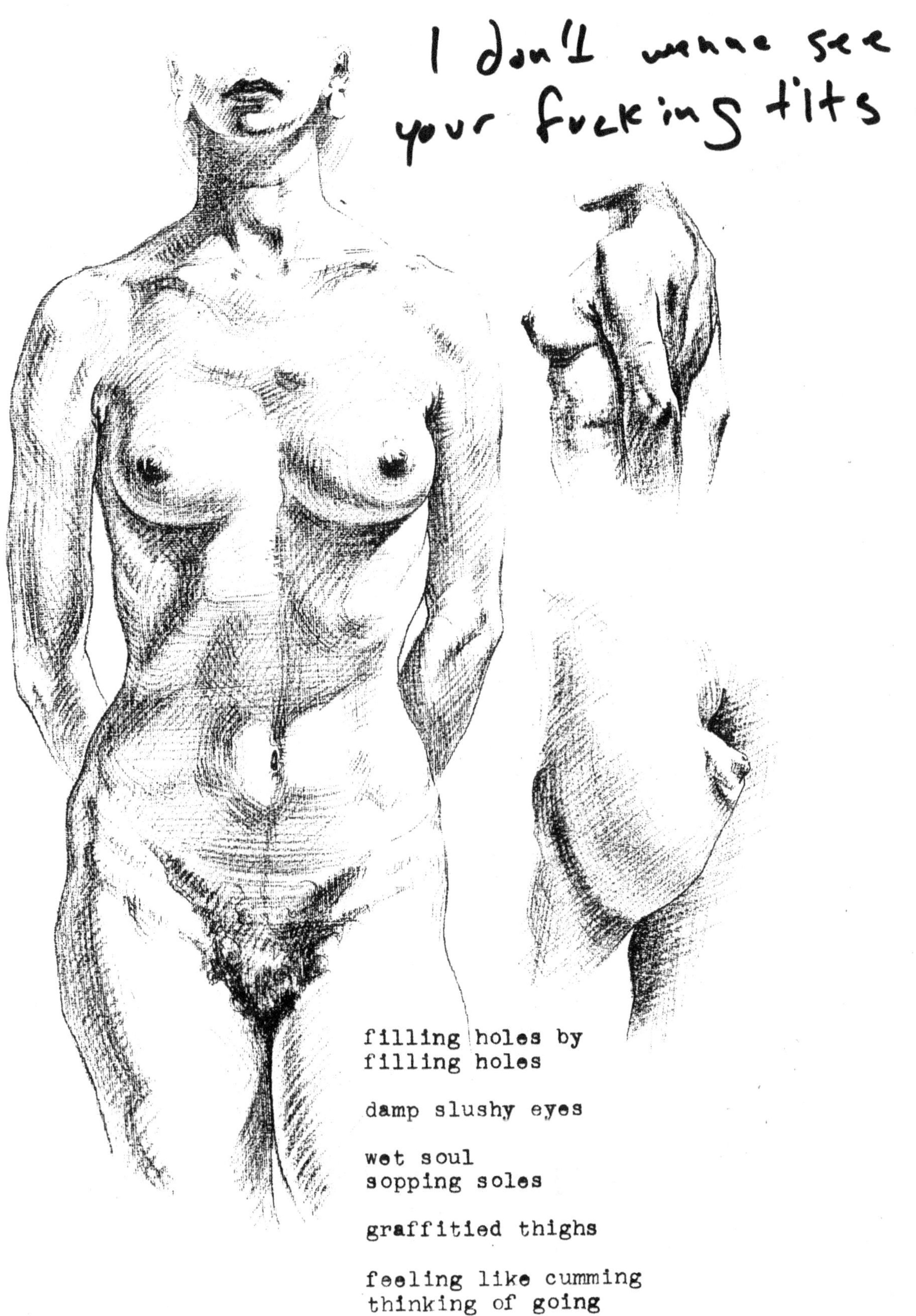

filling holes by
filling holes

damp slushy eyes

wet soul
sopping soles

graffitied thighs

feeling like cumming
thinking of going

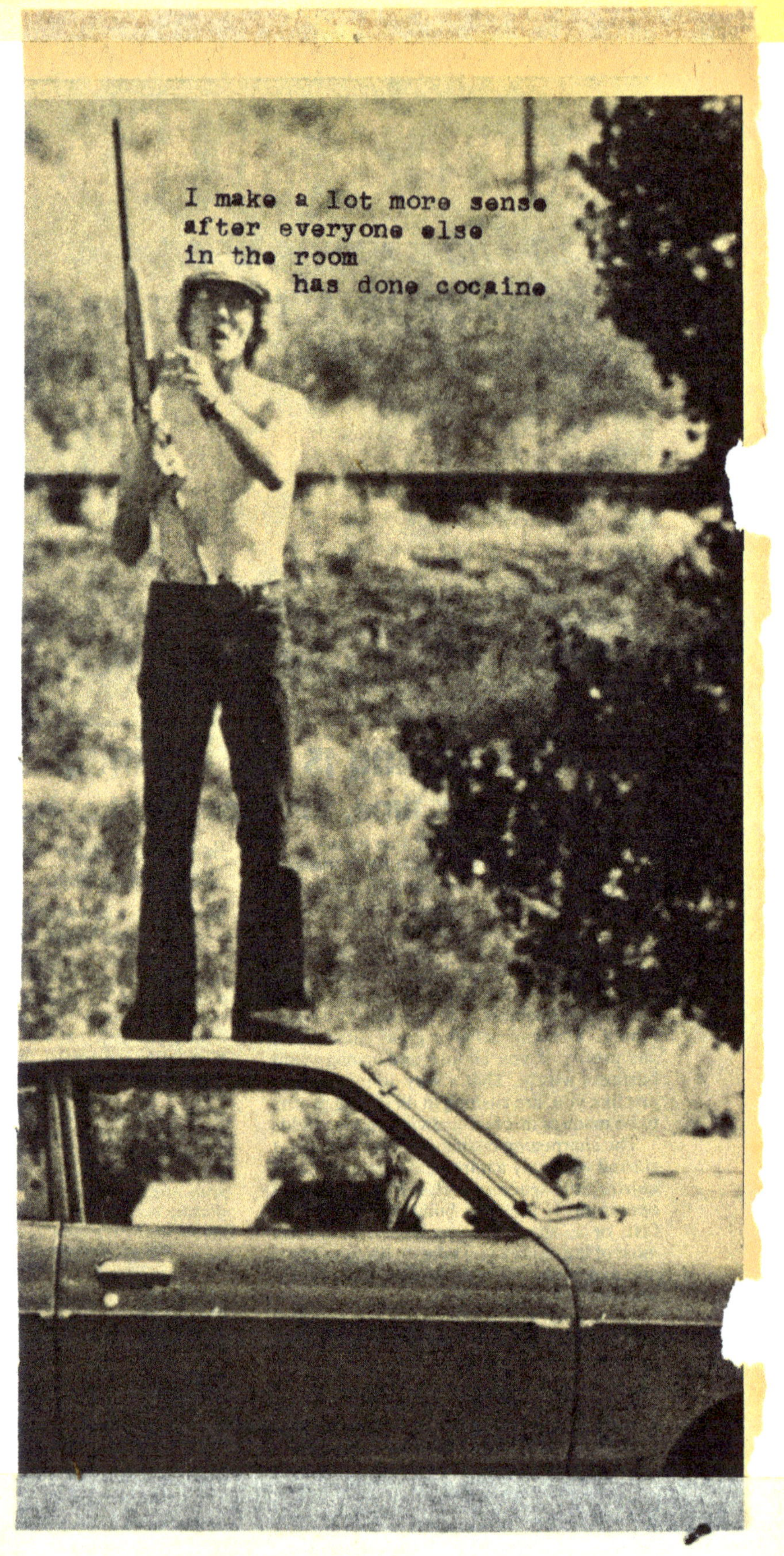
I make a lot more sense
after everyone else
in the room
has done cocaine

Sad bastard

I came home
drunk
and stoned
and wrote
something poignant
and beautiful
but
who cares?
no one
even cares
I got home

I;"'

I'm taking a shit
and doing coke
in a rather
disgusting ~~bathroom~~
of a dive bar that's
sunk into the ground
new ~~by~~ the Ala Moana
boat harbor
that smells like
burnt hair
~~and moldy mop head~~
wondering if I should
order nachos

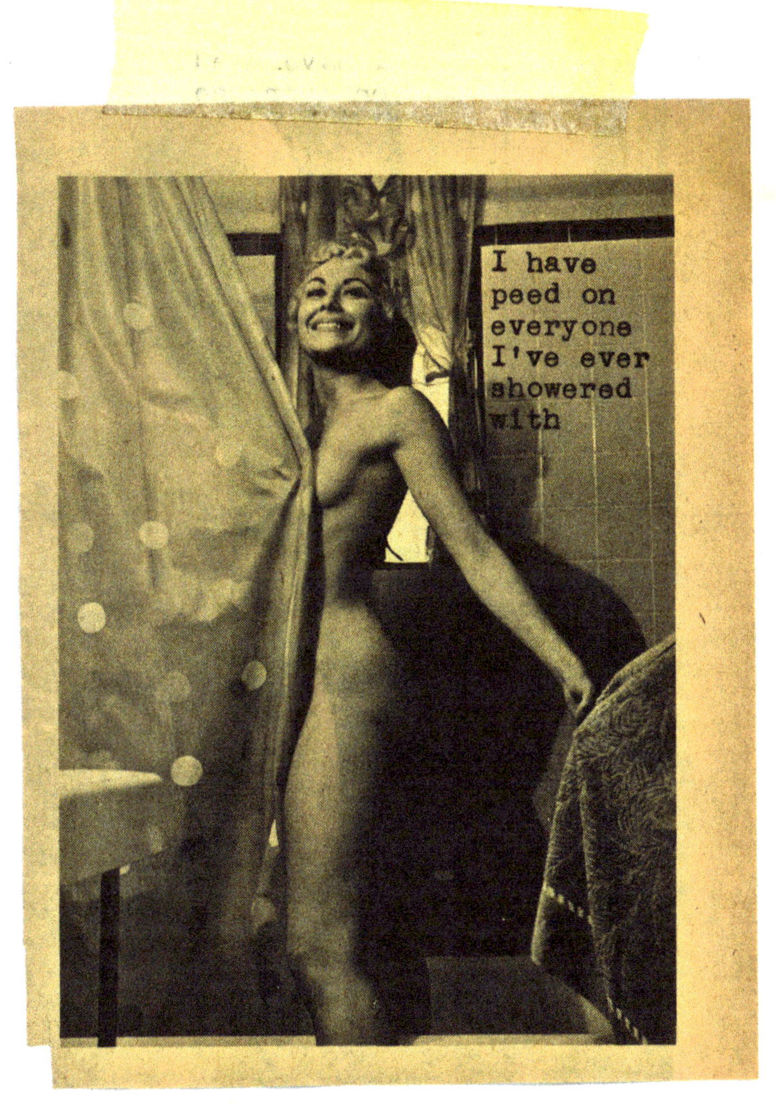
I have
peed on
everyone
I've ever
showered
with

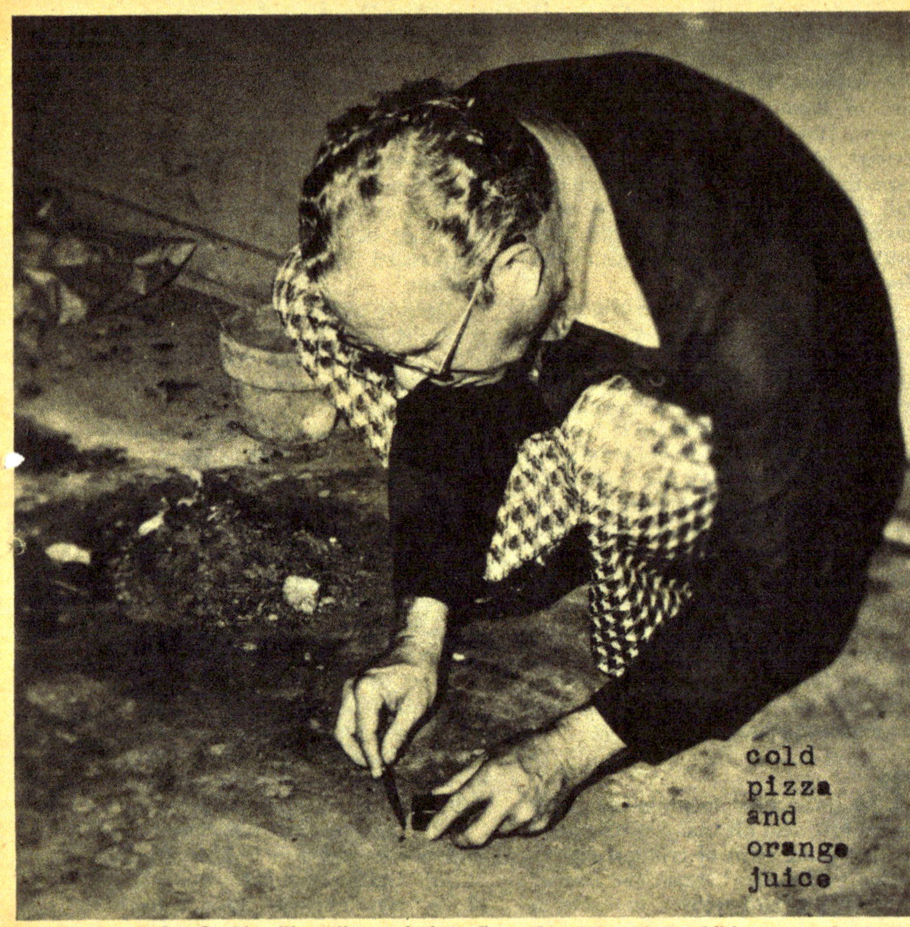

Sgt. Cushing lifts soil sample from floor of building where child was raped

town . . Stay on the sidewalks . . Children should tell parents their routes."

After it was determined that none of the five young girls who had been brought to headquarters could recognize any of the photographs in the mug books, officers decided to get written statements from them. While the statement...

went to Lookout Street in Attalla. A check at the Lookout Street address, cleared the suspect who lived there.

Officers had continued to comb the area of the site of the kidnaping. After the Attalla lead proved to be false, Lt. Alexander and Officer Jeffers, together with

admit
earlier
young
Hall.
Taylo
store
there
Calhou
Street.
Cadilla
custod
of his r
taken.
409 All

Wh
was bei
event w
found v
Gadsde
Street.
"When
daylight
and sho
Sam put
back do
to three,
and you
When yo
and you

Tracy
rememb
I started
started a
house an
if I coul
number
brother.
gave hin
father c
mother, a
quarters.'

Tracy
the search
and it we
with her c

At city
ghastly ev

sked one of the

the frightened

said.
etly.
ement to police
, "We cut off
hind a building
oad and a house
he boys told me
I told him, 'no.'

e car passed by
decided to walk
vo men and the
Street, a main
y, "We went to
went in behind
s not stop here,'
m the back of a
. We stopped
,' then we went
e graveyard to
Street."
old abandoned
cy stated that,
they took me in-
l me to take my
rizing the child
Tracy said, "He
e other boy was
Then he got on
me one time.
'I'm fixing to go
de is finished at
ther boy raped
during each at-
the assailant to
isten.
irst man return-
eliminary hear-

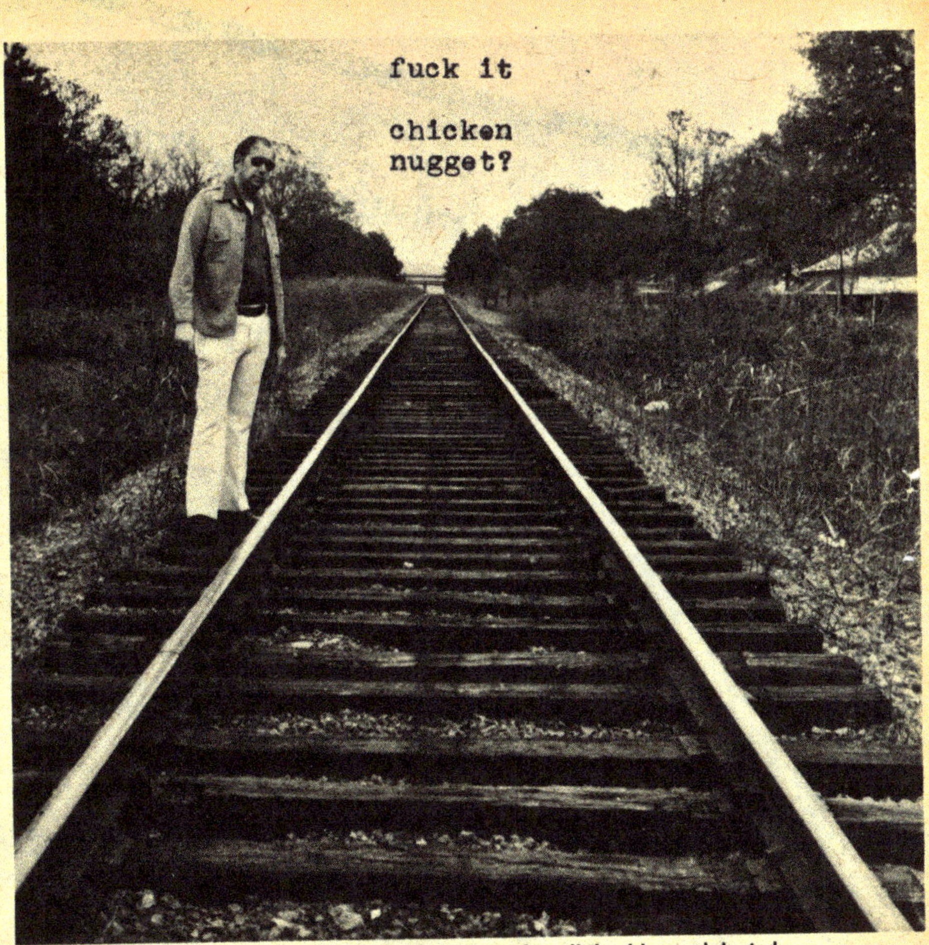

Det. Sgt. Couch, now deceased, stands at spot where little girl was abducted

ran off the nearest trail to seek assistance.

and Tracy's three companions to the city

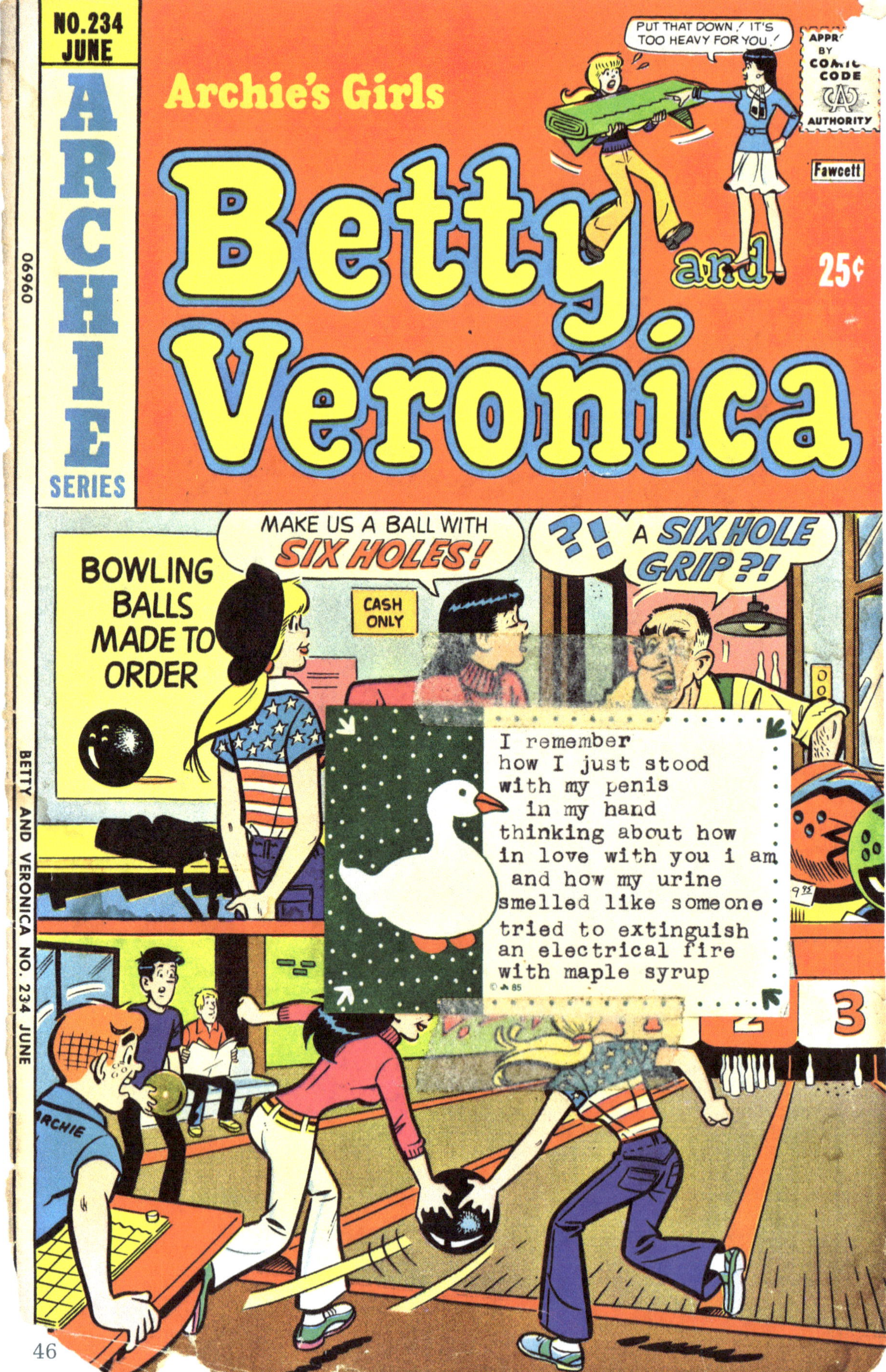
NO. 234
JUNE
ARCHIE
SERIES
Archie's Girls
Betty and Veronica
PUT THAT DOWN! IT'S TOO HEAVY FOR YOU!
Fawcett
25¢
06960
BETTY AND VERONICA NO. 234 JUNE
BOWLING BALLS MADE TO ORDER
MAKE US A BALL WITH SIX HOLES!
CASH ONLY
?! A SIX HOLE GRIP?!
ARCHIE
3
I remember
how I just stood
with my penis
in my hand
thinking about how
in love with you i am
and how my urine
smelled like someone
tried to extinguish
an electrical fire
with maple syrup

he Leg

ke the arms, the two sections of the g are modified cylindrical shapes, but e even longer and heavier than the ns. The major difference is that the nts of the arms and legs are hinged opposite directions. Otherwise, the me approach can be followed when awing the arms and legs, visualizing em first as glass tumblers. Once you ve determined the degree of fore-ortening involved in the position of ch section, you can easily modify the lindrical shapes to resemble the con-urs of the limbs.

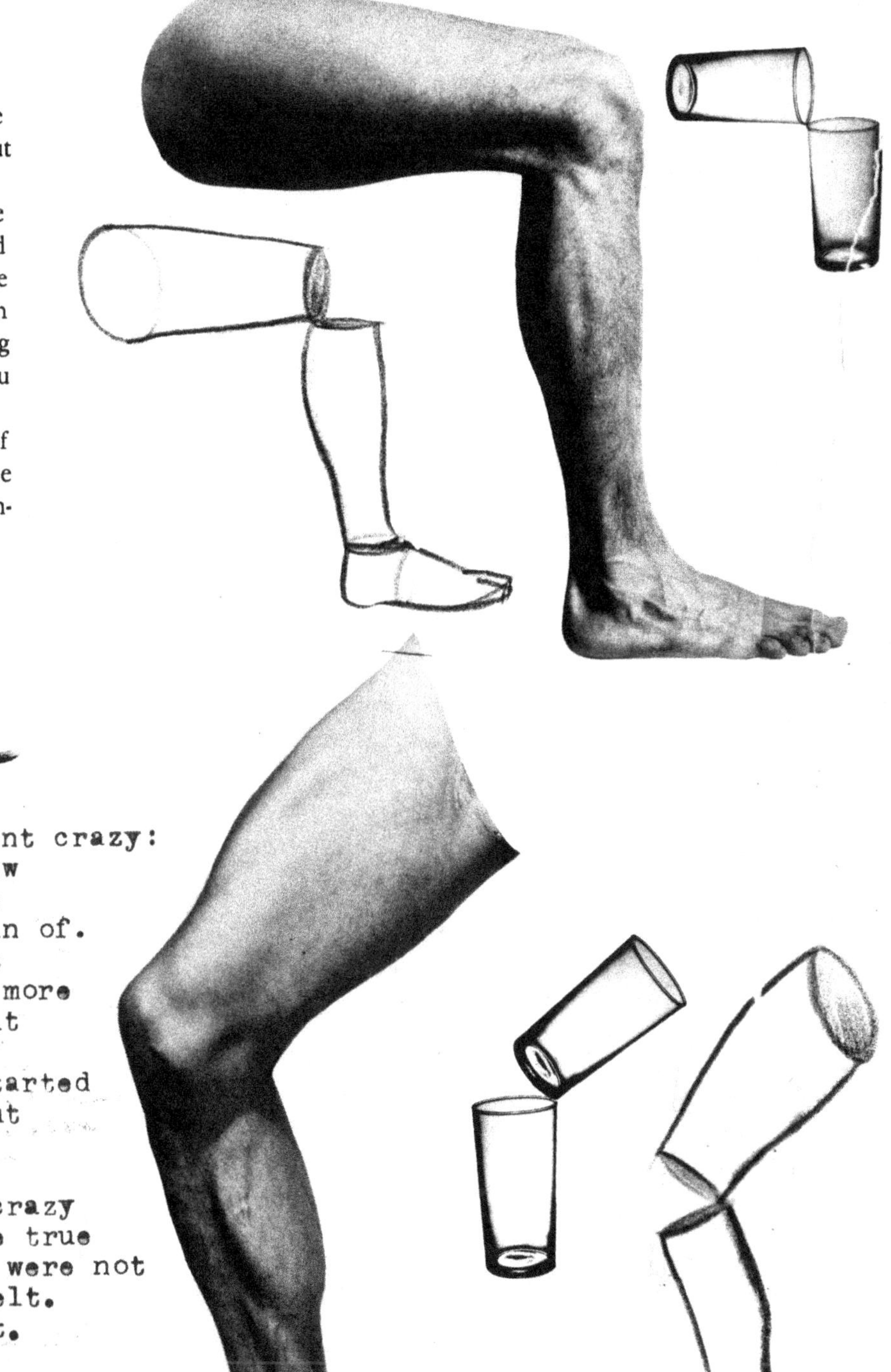

tease

Here's where I went crazy:
It was when I knew
I was feelin more
than I was thinkin of.
Wasn't the moment
I started feelin more
than I knew I felt
anything about.
Or even when I started
thinkin more about
what I thought
about knowing.
I knew I'd gone crazy
when I knew to be true
things I thought were not
cause of how I felt.
I fucking knew it.

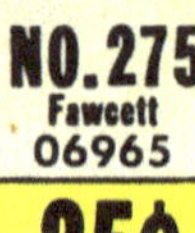

35¢

ARCHIE SERIES

APPROVED BY THE COMICS CODE AUTHORITY

Archie

ARCHIE, WHAT'S THE SCORE?

ER, SO FAR IT'S TWELVE BRUNETTES TO NINE BLONDES!

ARCHIE NO.275

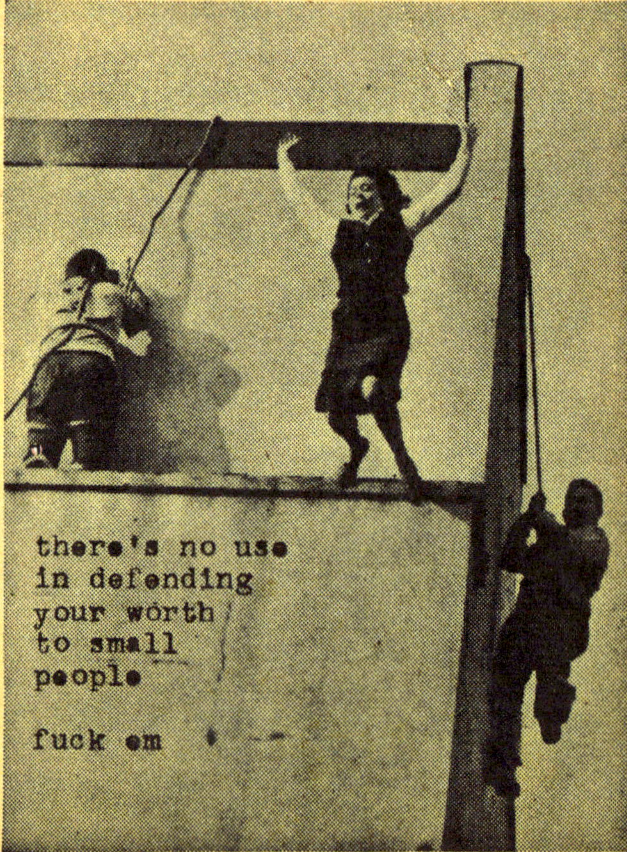

48

27

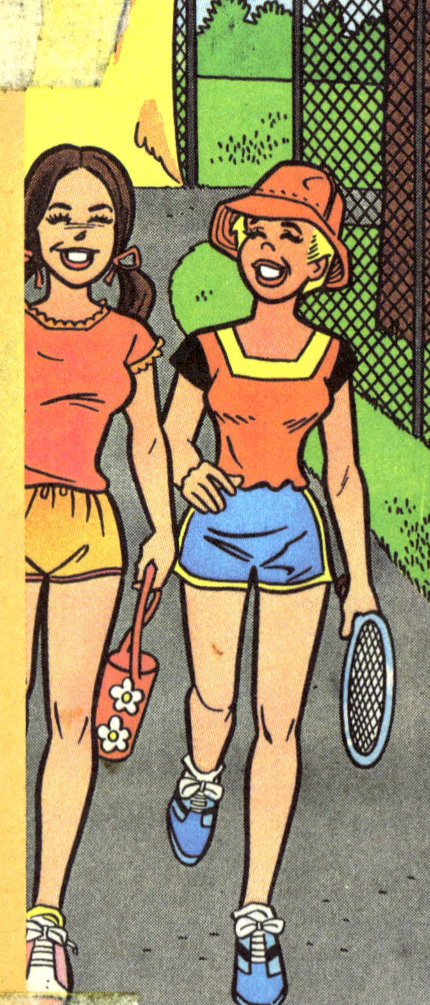

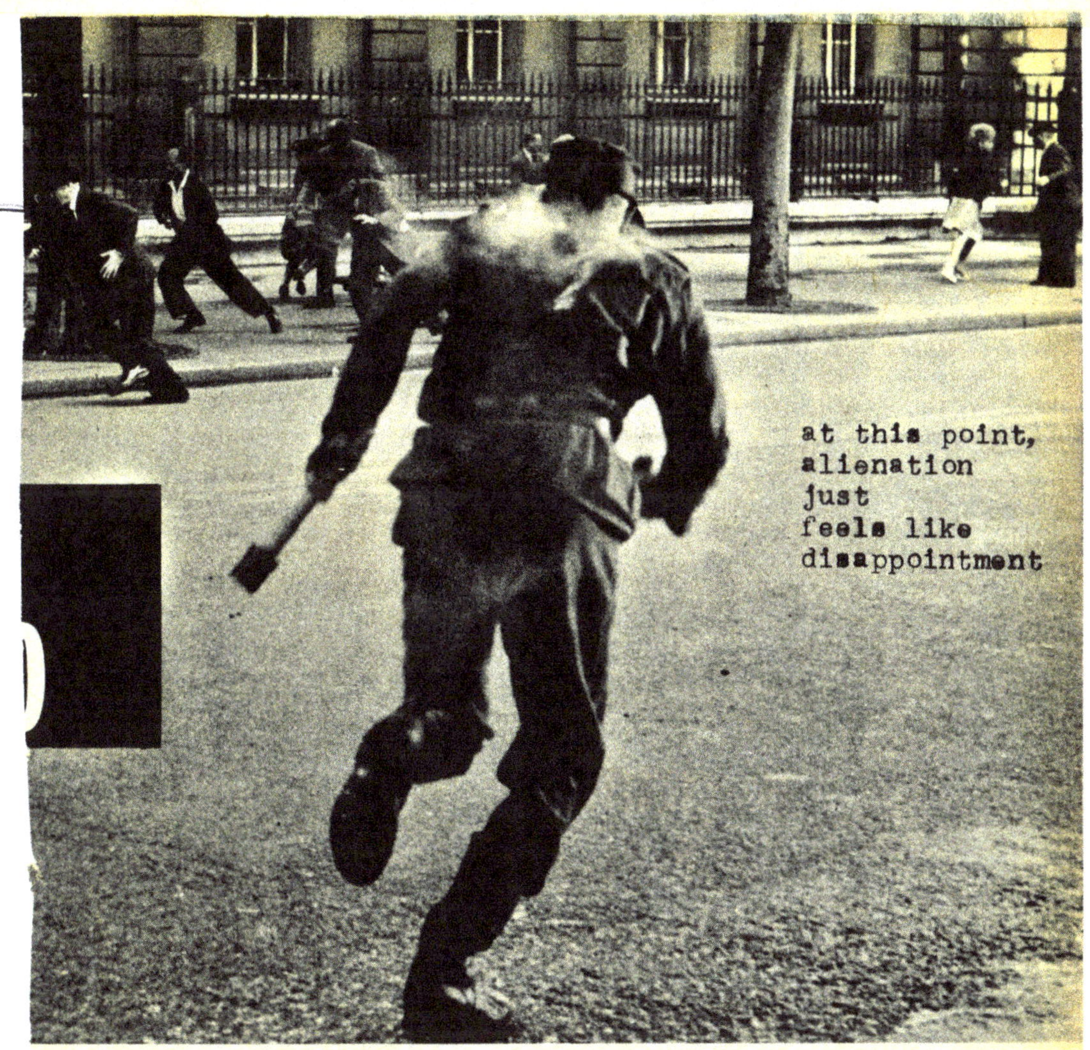
at this point,
alienation
just
feels like
disappointment
etta with Gromek traced back to latter's WW II activities when he bossed
ed civilians indiscriminately (above). Gromek was feared throughout Europe

Transfer Function)
ing the sharpness of
on a graph the ratio
ontrast against the
To the experienced
tains more
lens quality than a
f resolution figures.

r
for a type of
paper, used to print
ng degrees of
of changing filters
his variation is made
grade's special
has a mixture of two
LIDE, one sensitive to
er to green light.
-sensitive part
ontrast image;
n-sensitive part
ntrast image. Yellow
absorb blue light and
agenta filters to
transmit blue. An
lour-mixing head can
n Multigrade paper,
l is possible with
e filters, which come
densities of yellow
, of course, also
n Multigrade using
ltigrade paper is of
age to photographers
reat deal of printing,
grades of paper were
d ones would tend to
useful for printing
, as by skilful local
ing of filters it is
art of the image
paper and part of it
rasty paper. Other
a similar product
name. Kodak's paper,
led 'Polycontrast'.

ra
g three or more
f exposure control) –
riority, shutter

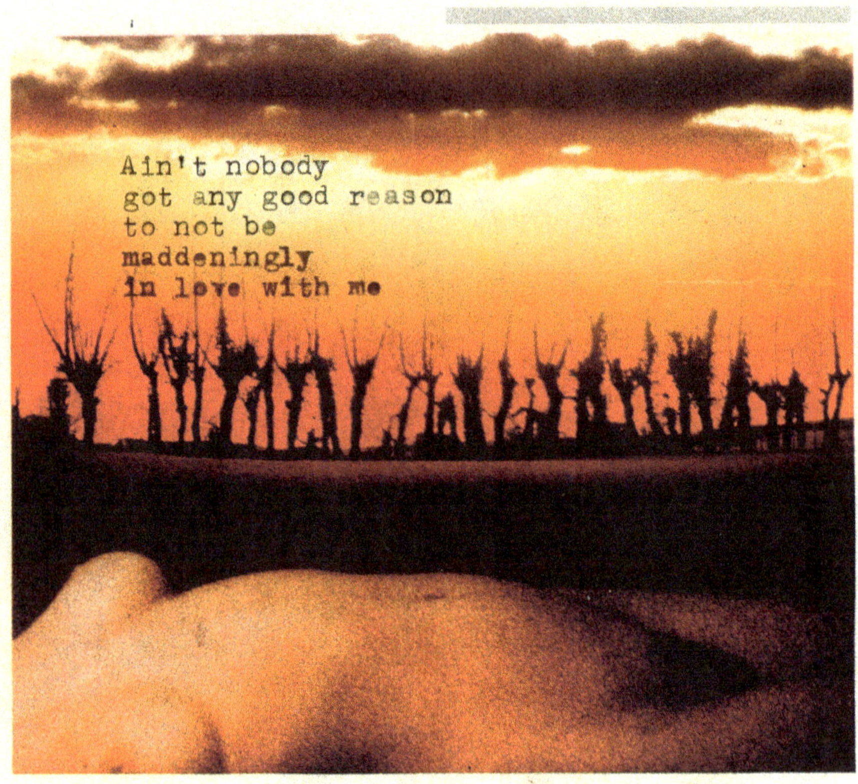

MONTAGE

priority and 'programmed' being the most common (see AUTOMATIC EXPOSURE). Multi-mode cameras require extremely sophisticated electronics, and are a recent innovation, the first – the Minolta XD7 – being introduced in 1977. The Canon T90, introduced in 1986, offers the most modes of any camera to date – manual, stopped-down manual, shutter priority, aperture priority, stopped-down AE, flash AE, and seven variable shift programs. Multi-mode cameras are relatively expensive, but because of their versatility already are very popular.

Multiple exposure see also CHROMOGRAPHOSCOPE, and under IVES, FREDERICK
Technique of establishing two or more images on one frame of film. Most cameras, but not all, make provision for multiple exposures so that a series of images may be recorded without winding on the film. Multiple exposure can also refer to several identical images on separate frames of film, and juxtaposed to make a composite image, as in the early colour cameras and viewers.

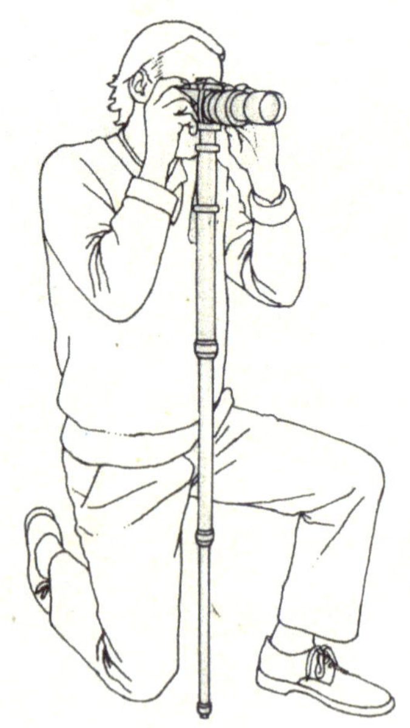

MONOPOD

Rising out of the smoke of battle, marines of the Black Sea Fleet counterattack near Tuapse, a Caucasian port at which the German advance toward Soviet oil fields was turned back. The feeling of frozen motion, so like a movie still, reflects Uzian's early training as a film maker.

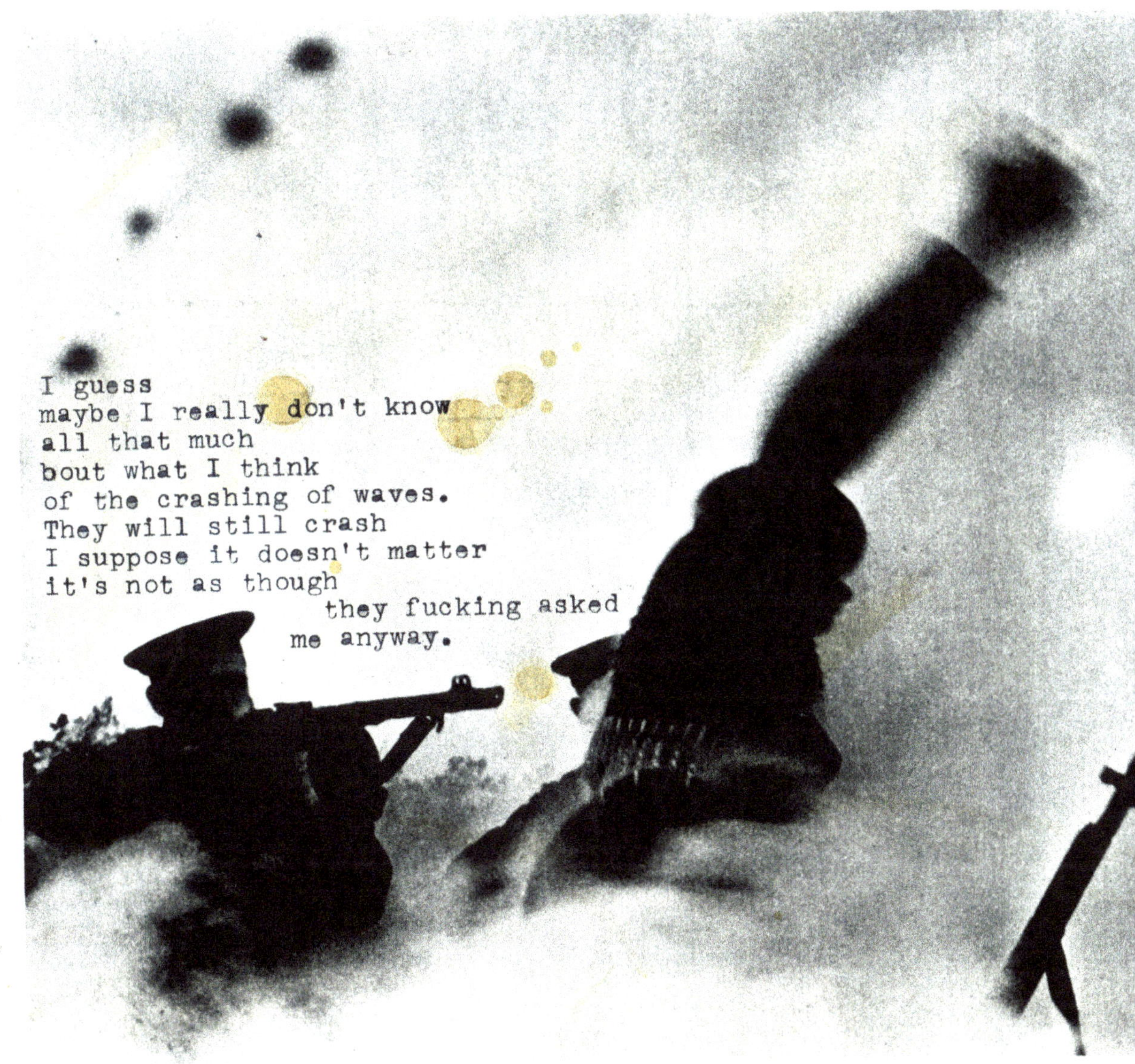

·LEXANDR UZIAN: *Black Sea Fleet,* 1942

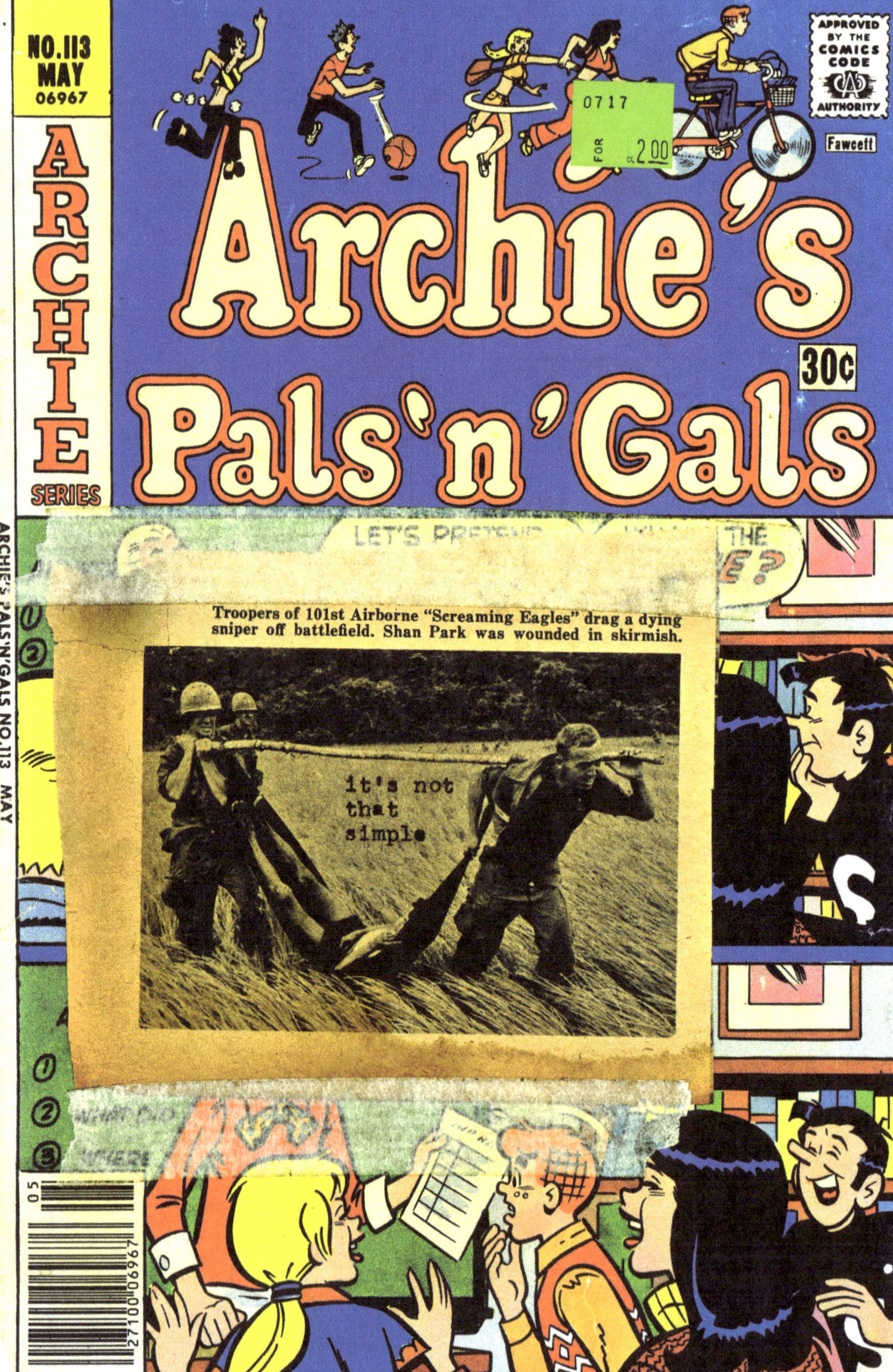
NO.113
MAY
06967
ARCHIE SERIES
APPROVED BY THE COMICS CODE AUTHORITY
Fawcett
0717
FOR
2.00
Archie's
Pals'n'Gals
30¢
ARCHIE'S PALS'N'GALS NO.113 MAY
Troopers of 101st Airborne "Screaming Eagles" drag a dying sniper off battlefield. Shan Park was wounded in skirmish.
it's not
that
simple
05
0 27100 06967

ndup

ıes

ıe LIFE's
·cord of
d in Los
ramatic
› South
rom the
w Guin-
›k Atoll
anding

›f dead
ıried in
ensors
ınd his
tion on
› lifted.
›lished
he na-
›t fam-
· in the

:ombat
ediacy
obtain.
wly es-
›osedly
hom he
› be not
a hand
ıis life—
hen the
hich he
›n take-
d to the
wave of

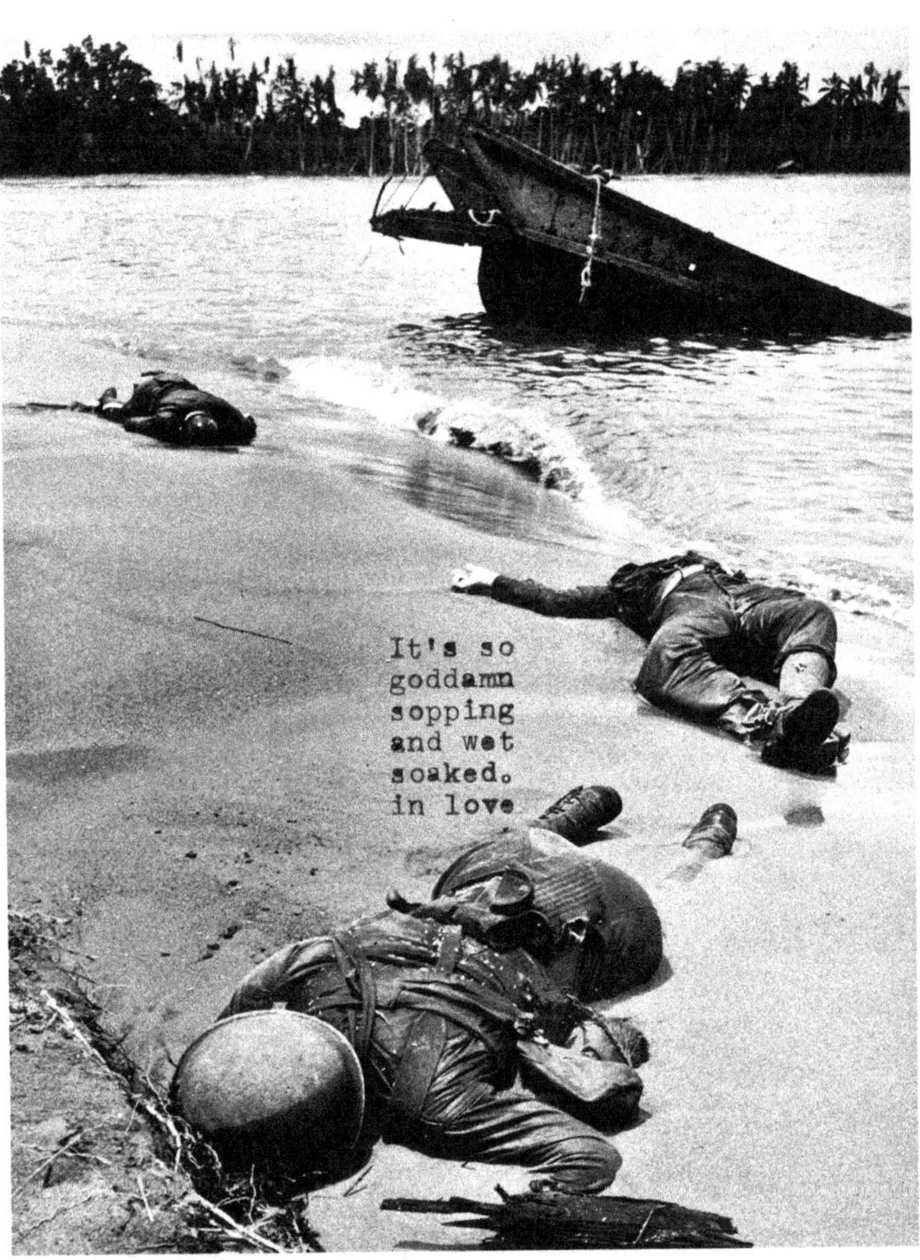

GEORGE STROCK: *Three Dead American Soldiers*, 1942

Strock got his start in 1934 taking fake-backdrop portraits in an amusement park and joined the LIFE staff in 1940. In his six years with the magazine and as a freelance afterward, he also covered political campaigns, Holly-

SHOCKING BOOK BONUS

Ransom for a Hot-Blooded Hook

"Racy...searing action...fast-paced story of a strange passion." (T

COMPLETE man

DEC. 35¢ 40¢ IN CANADA MAGAZINE

Confessions
A Vietcong Gue
"GI's A
TOO DA
TOUGH

TARGET OF U. S. CUSTOMS

BRA AND PANTY VICE GI

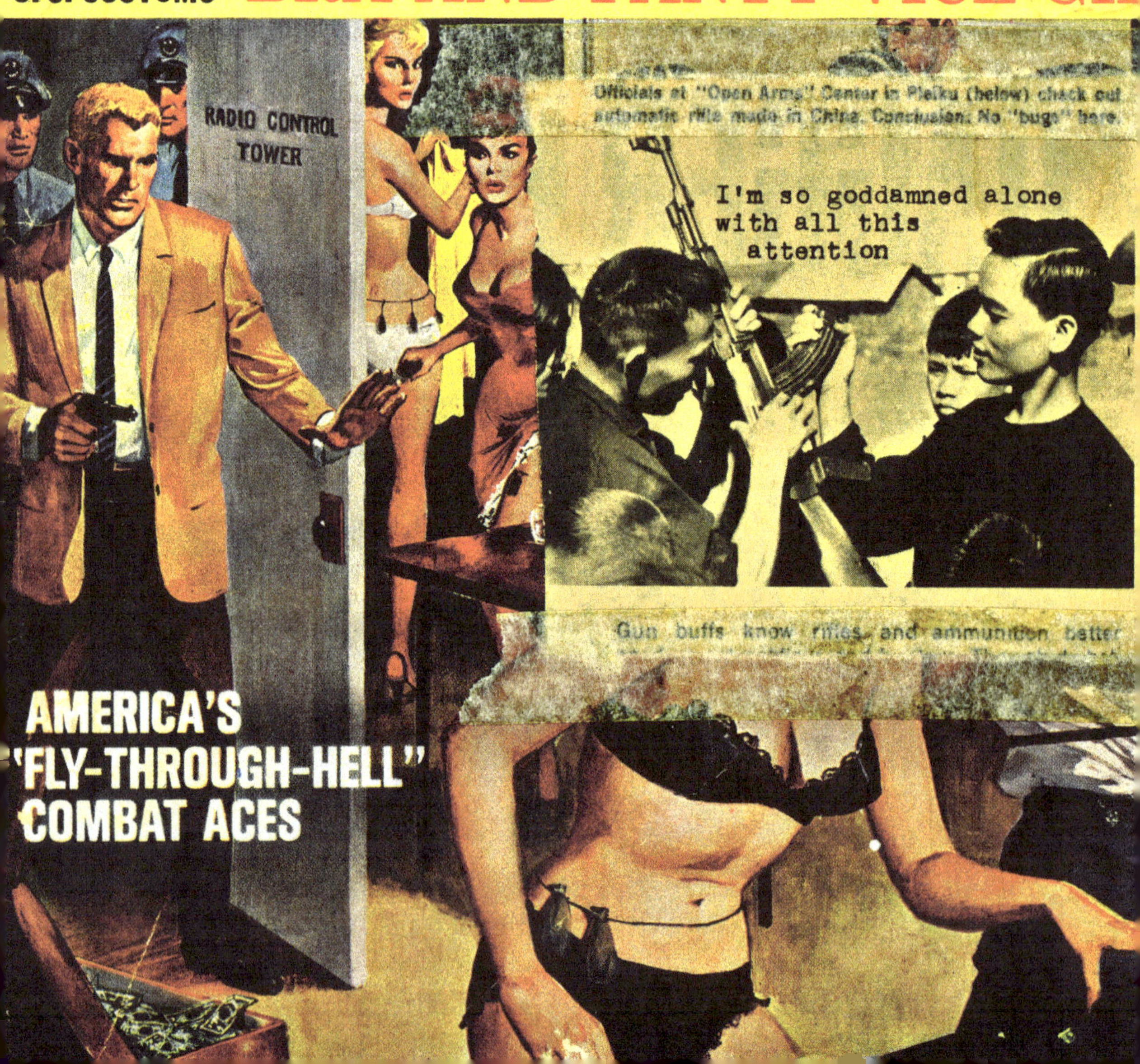

Date

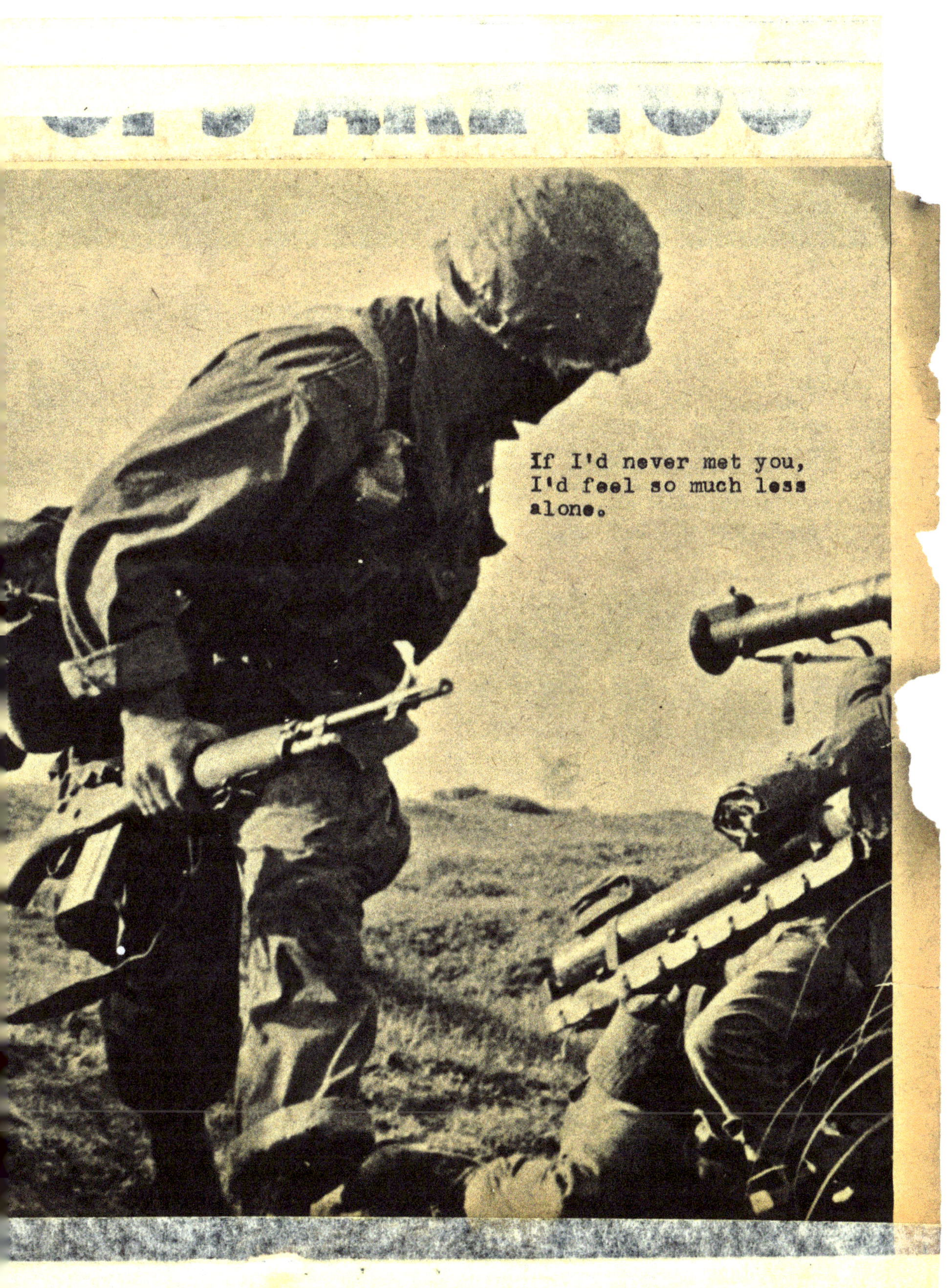

Page

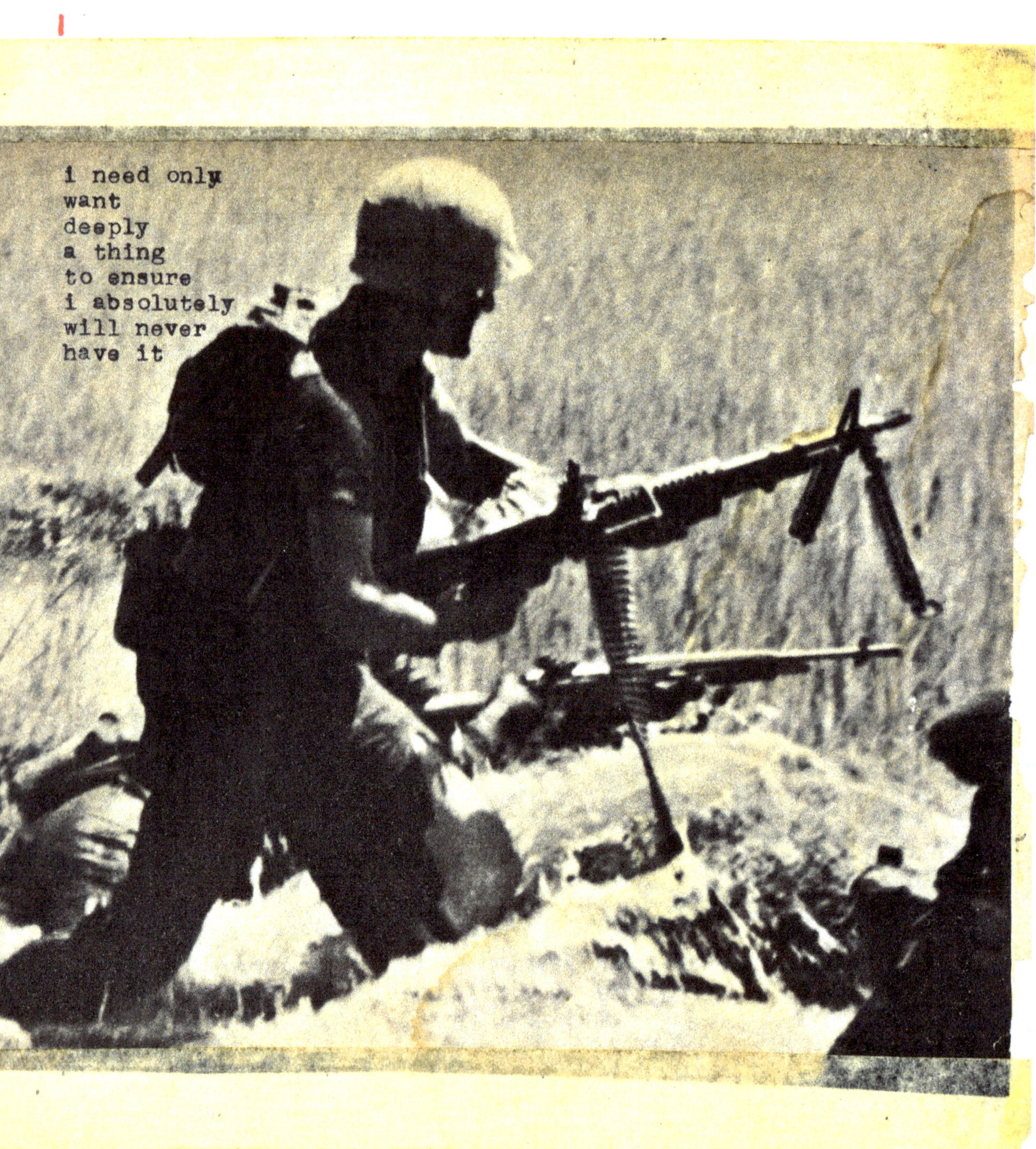
i need only
want
deeply
a thing
to ensure
i absolutely
will never
have it

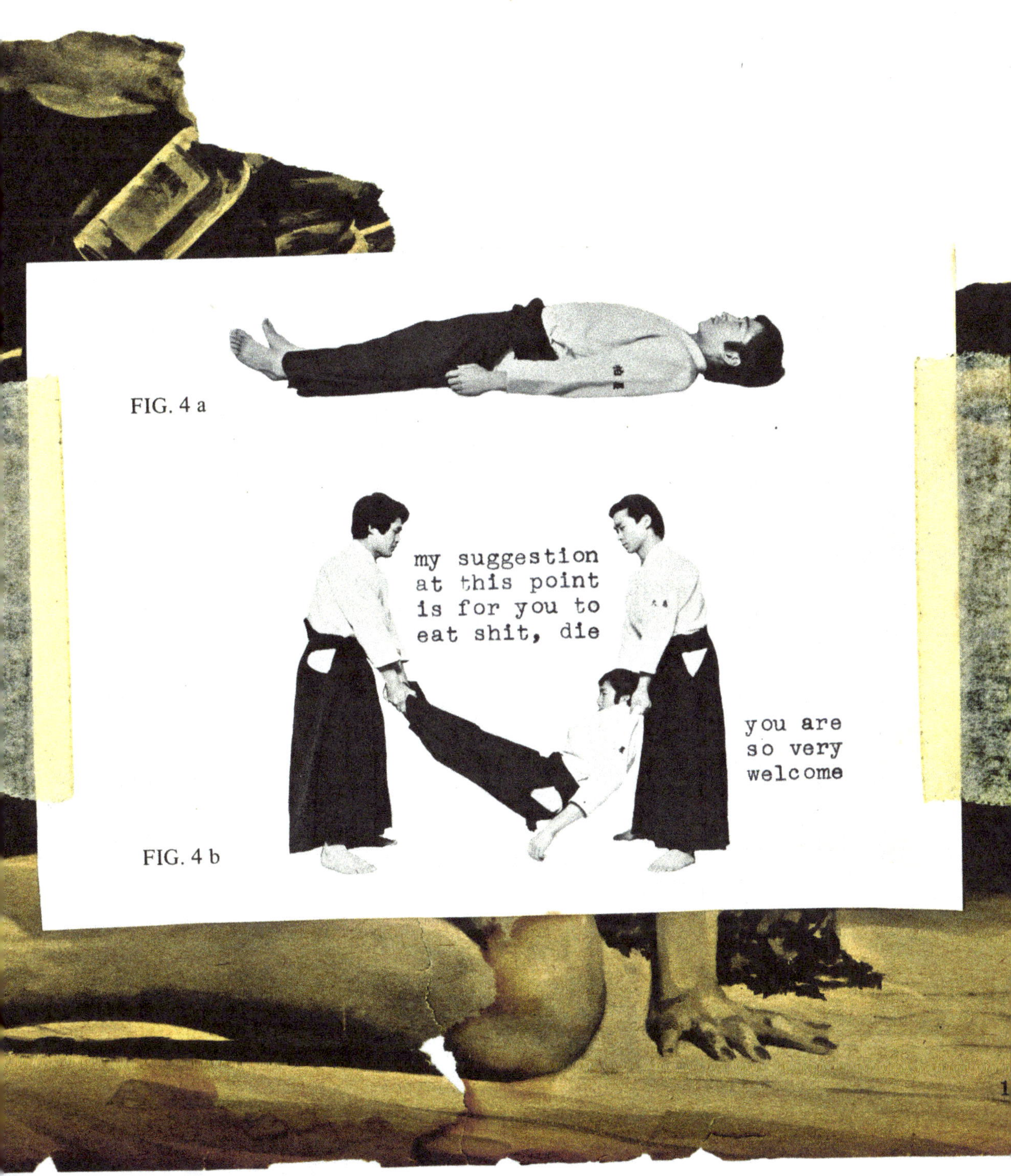
FIG. 4 a
my suggestion
at this point
is for you to
eat shit, die
you are
so very
welcome
FIG. 4 b

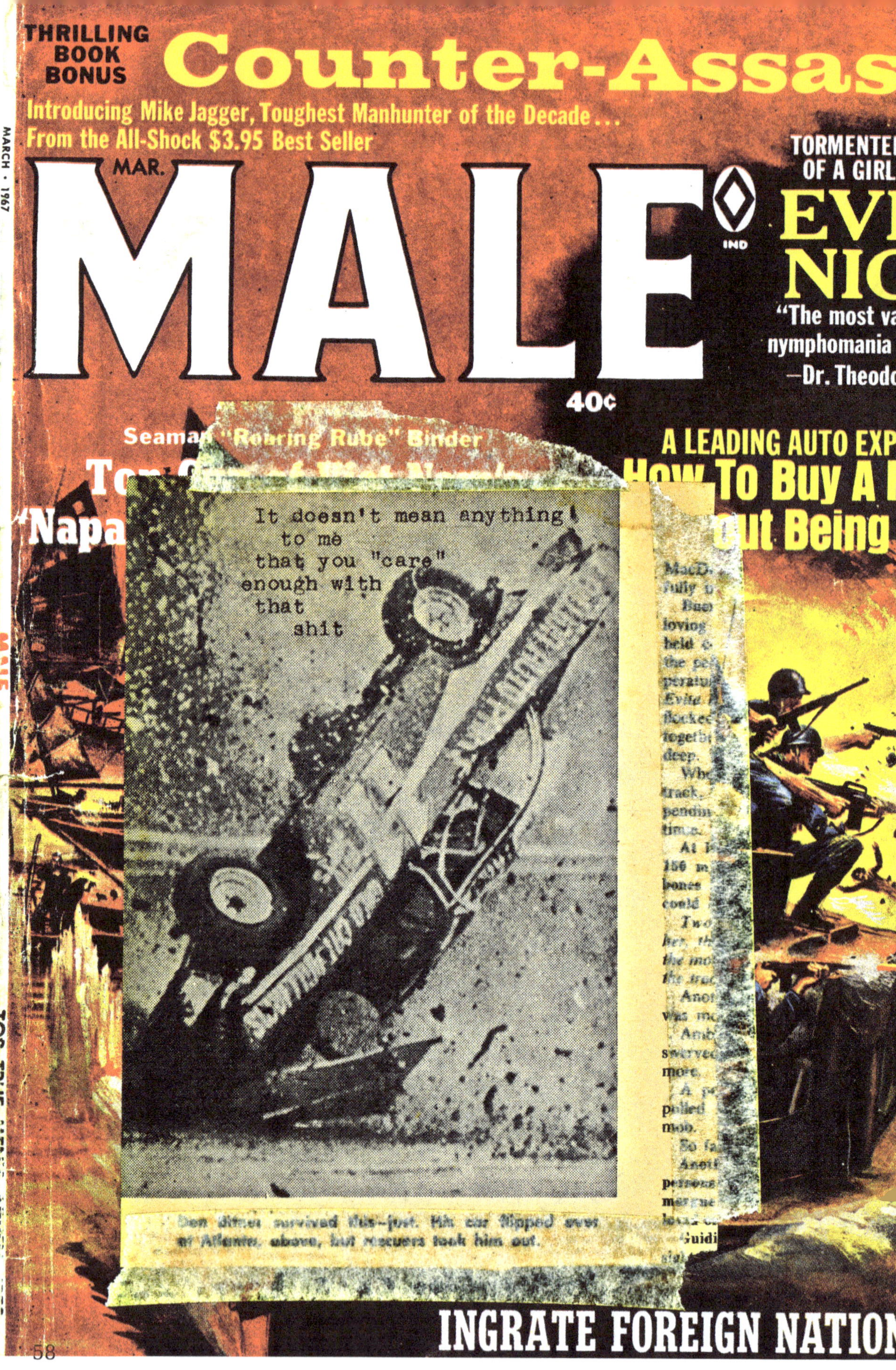

THRILLING BOOK BONUS
Counter-Assas
Introducing Mike Jagger, Toughest Manhunter of the Decade...
From the All-Shock $3.95 Best Seller
MARCH · 1967
MAR.
MALE
IND
40¢
TORMENTED
OF A GIRL
EV
NIC
"The most va
nymphomania
—Dr. Theodo
Seaman "Roaring Rube" Binder
'Napa
A LEADING AUTO EXP
How To Buy A N
out Being
It doesn't mean anything
to me
that you "care"
enough with
that
shit
MALE
TOP TRUE MEN'S ADVEN
INGRATE FOREIGN NATION

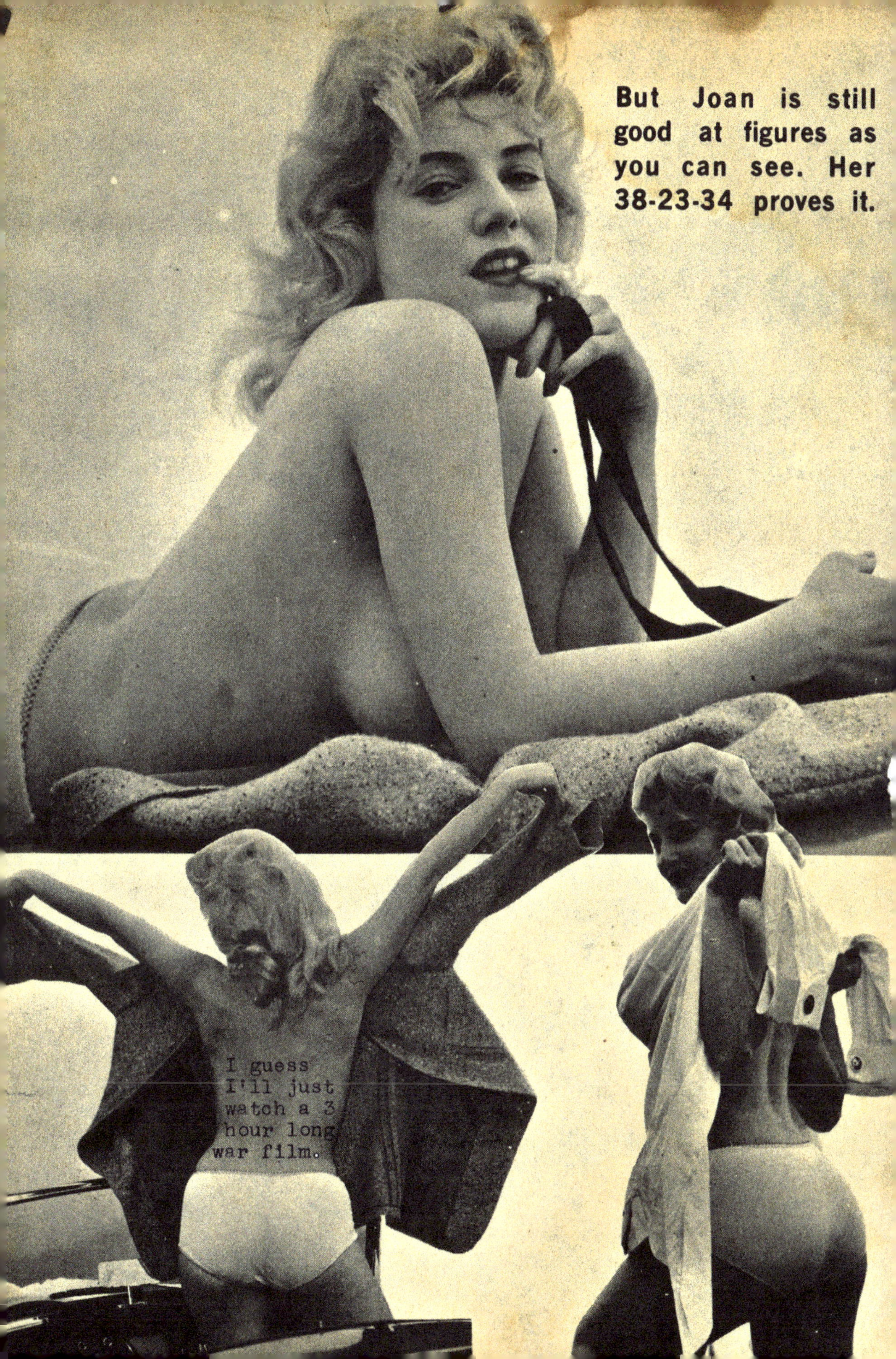

But Joan is still good at figures as you can see. Her 38-23-34 proves it.

honkey

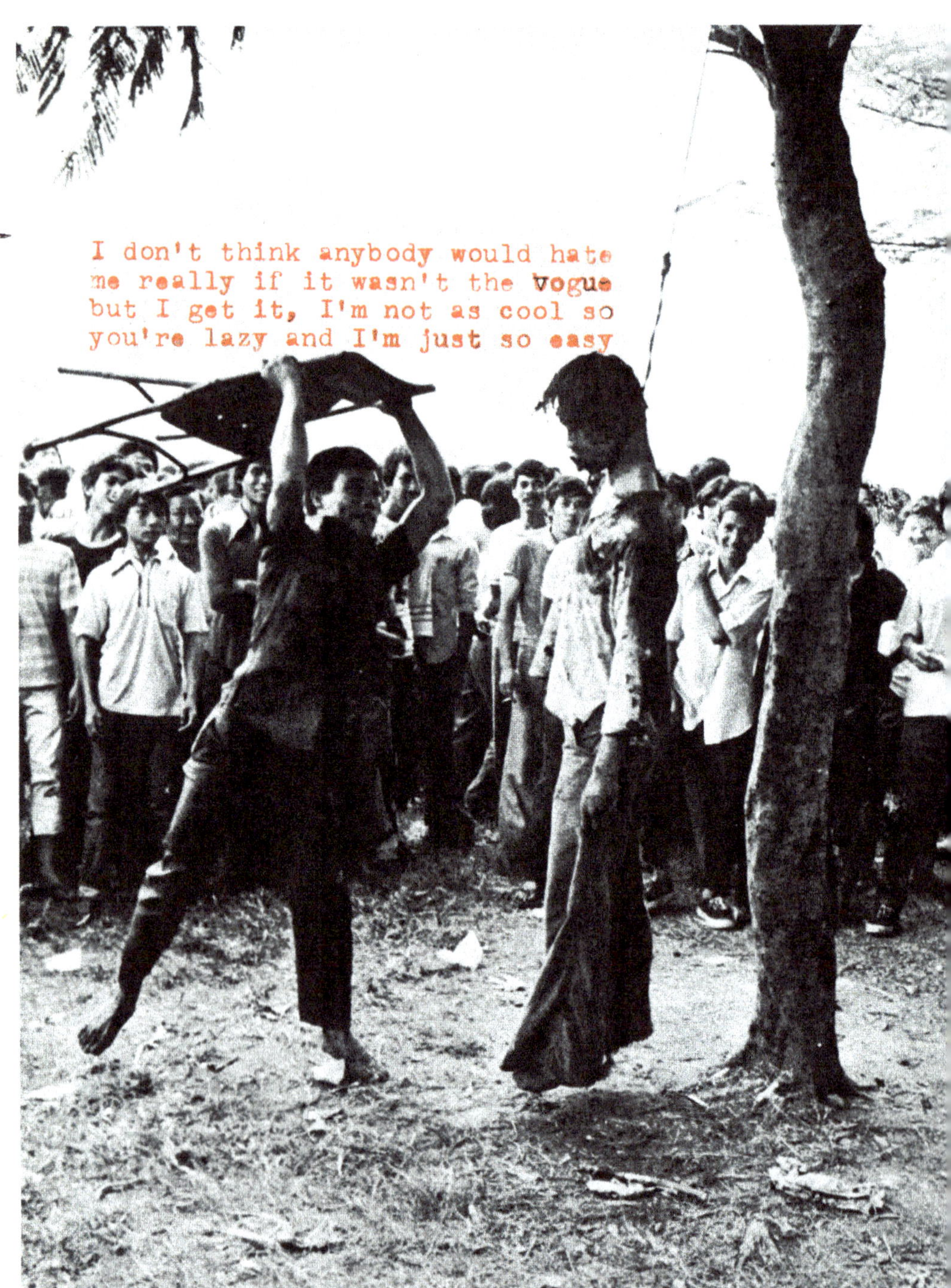

NEAL ULEVICH: *Brutality in Bangkok*, 1976

r Spot News
U.S.A.

age, a white youth wielding
black lawyer passing
an antibussing demonstration
icture earned Forman, a
he Boston Herald American, his
itzer. This year he shares the
an Associated Press
cited for his coverage of the
nstrations in Thailand,
h at right of a young rightist
mmunist student with a chair.

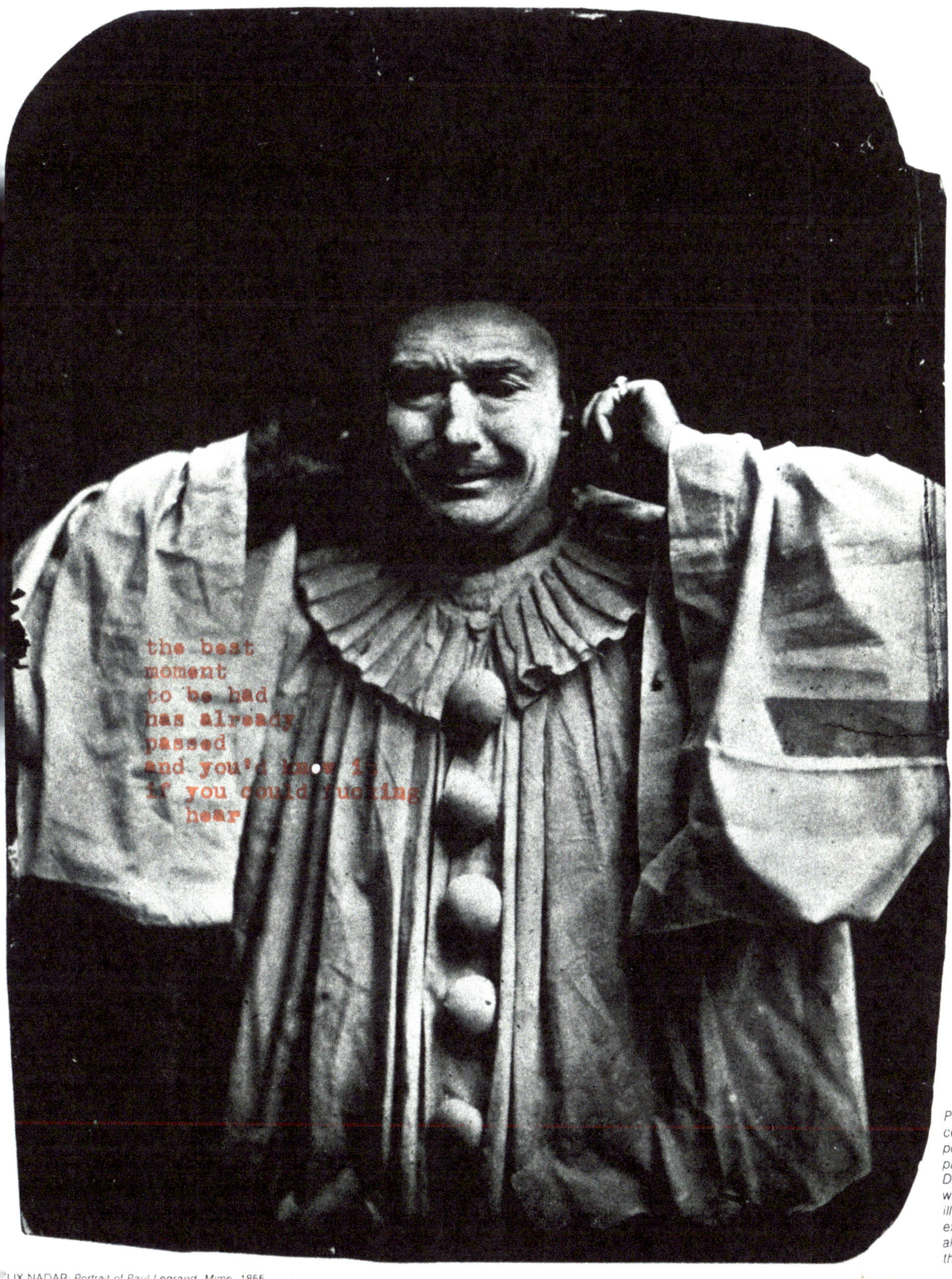

'LIX NADAR *Portrait of Paul Legrand, Mime*, 1855

Paul Le
celebrit
portraiti
partly to
Duchen
who pub
illustrati
express
album a
this one

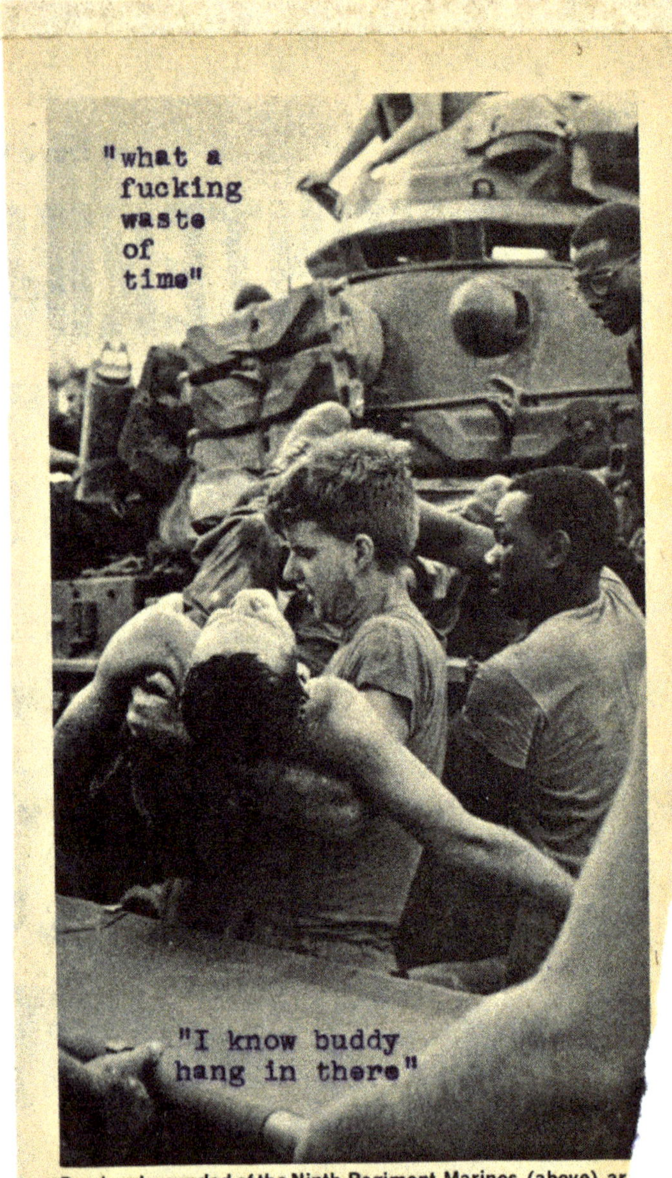

Dead and wounded of the Ninth Regiment Marines (above) ar
loaded onto tanks at DMZ. Noone knows how many casualti
have resulted from inefficient weapon. Photo below

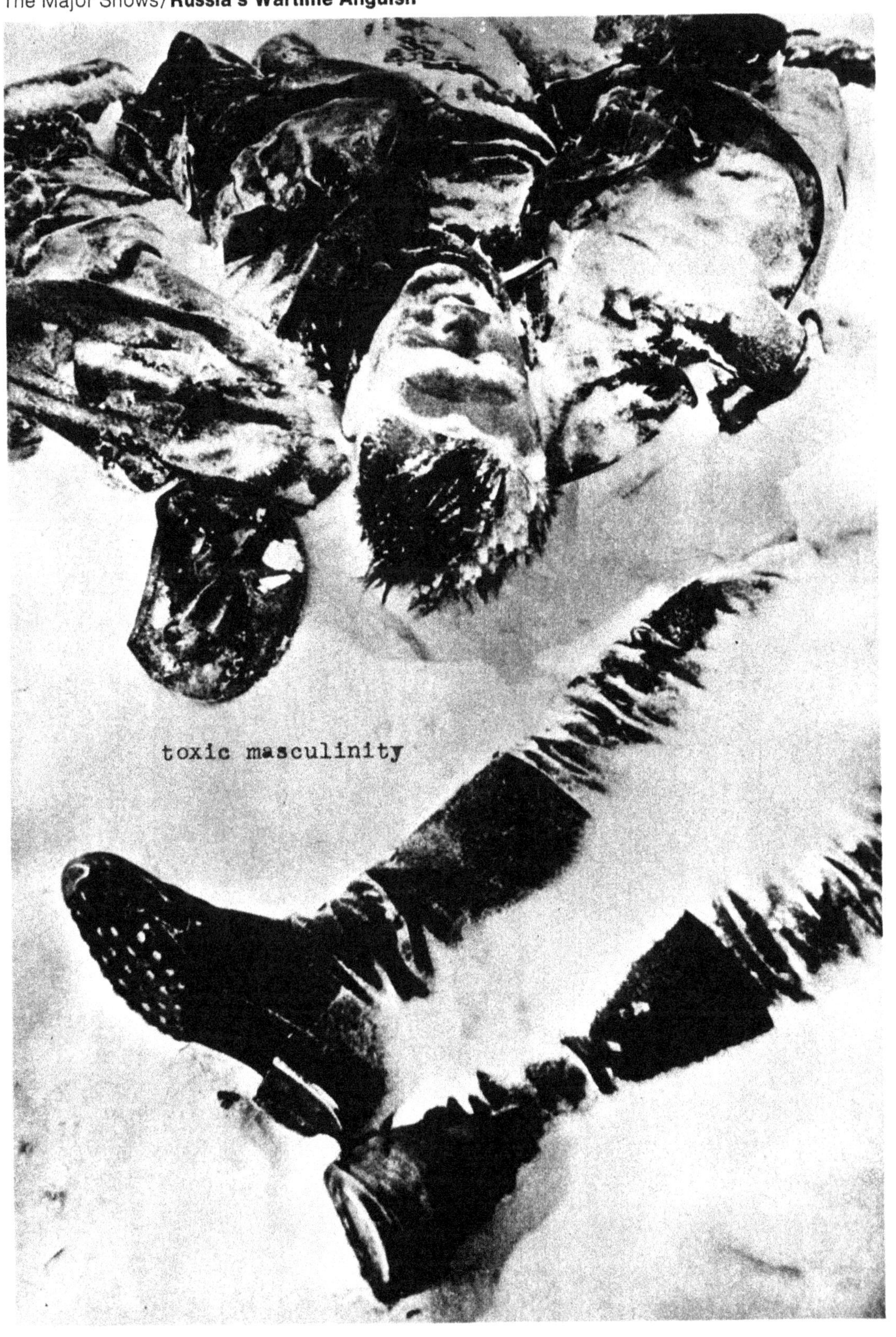

This g
corpse
soldie
from t
who c
the ou
Russia

GALINA SANKOVA: *On Russian Soil*, 1941

Date

PENTAGON SNAFU

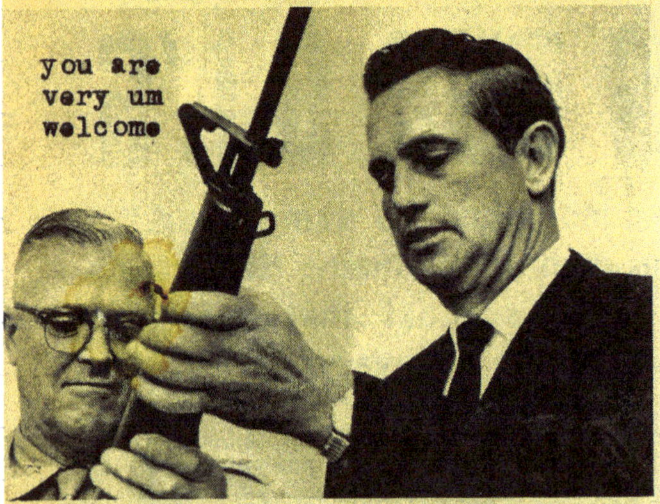

you are
very um
welcome

Rep. Richard Ichord examines M-16 with Maj. Gen. W.J. Van Ryzin. Ichord's report blasts military and two private firms.

Date

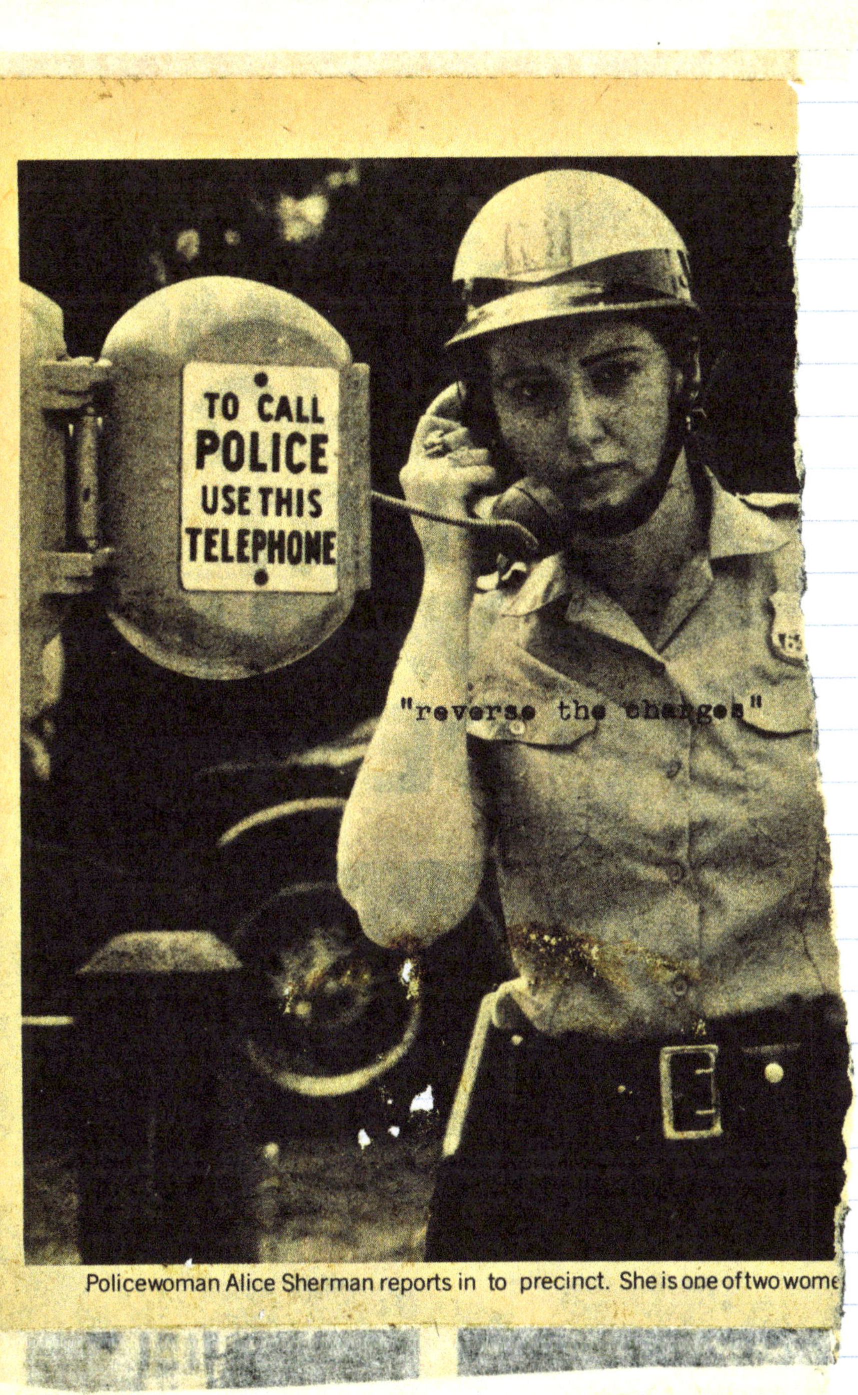

Policewoman Alice Sherman reports in to precinct. She is one of two wome

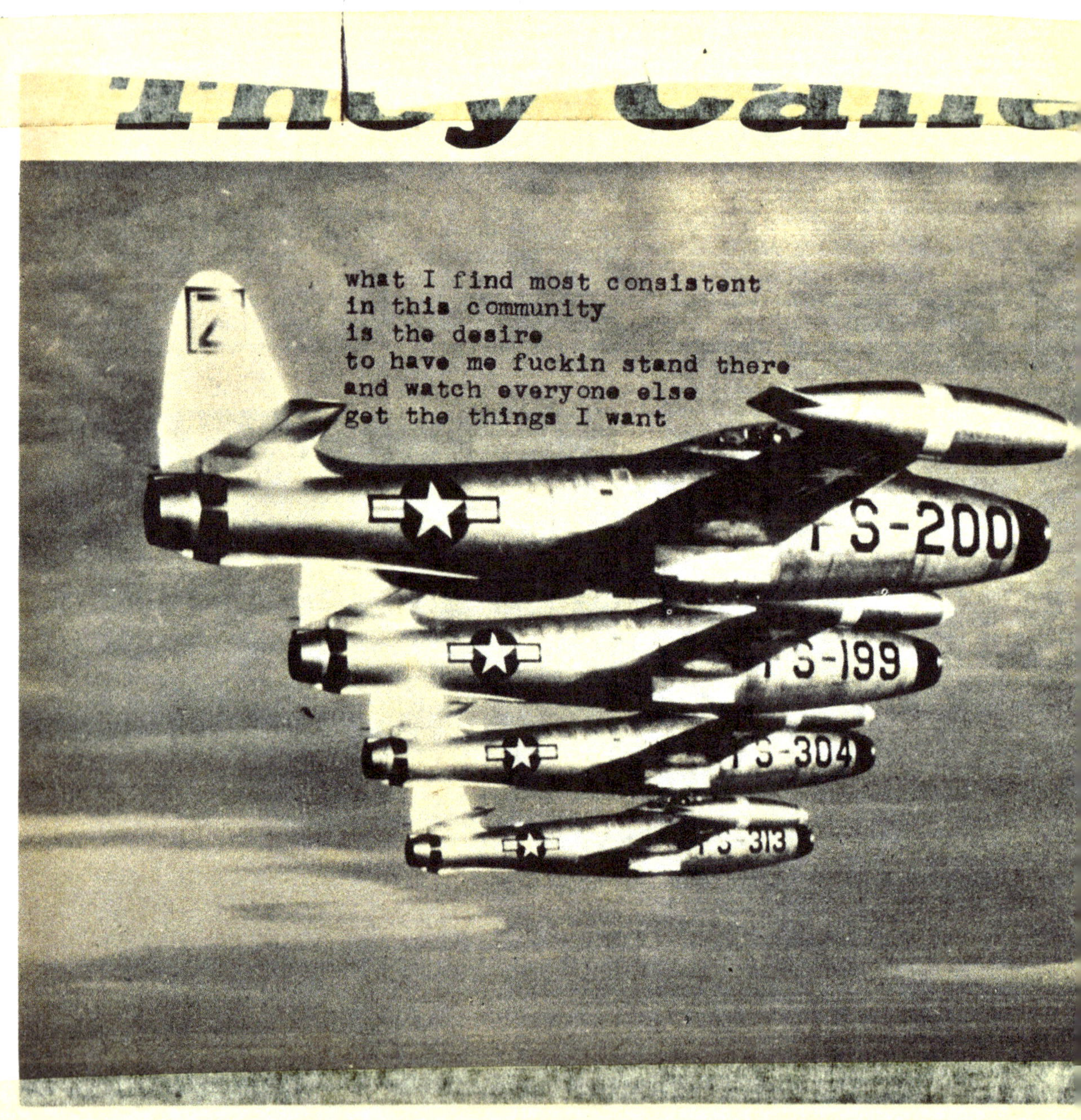
what I find most consistent
in this community
is the desire
to have me fuckin stand there
and watch everyone else
get the things I want
FS-200
FS-199
FS-304

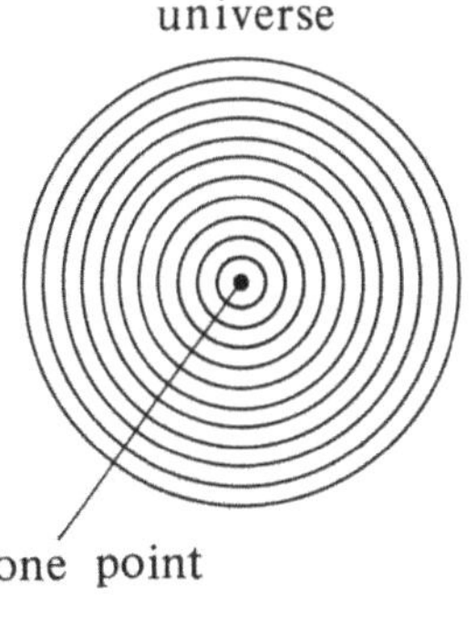

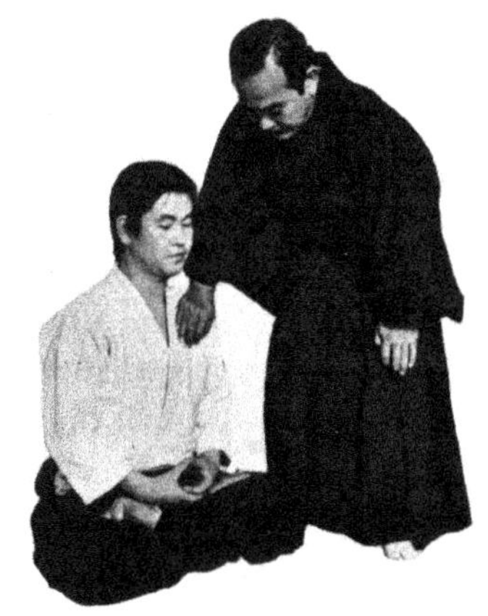

FIG. 9

most people don't do anything
but it's just not their fault

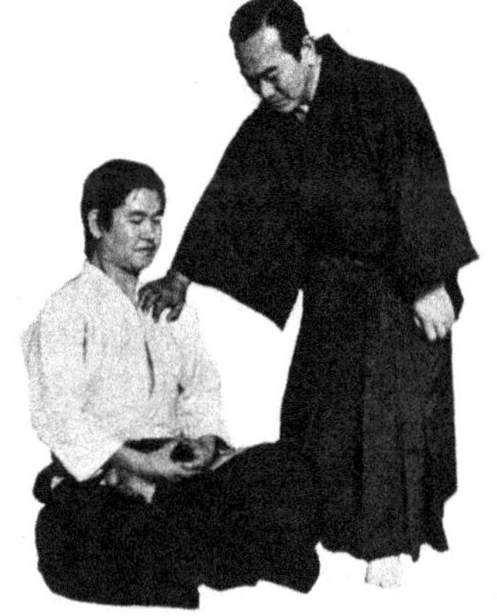

they need to deceive you
to feel like they matter

FIG. 10

has become small enough," or "I have accomplished the unification of mind and body." Even though he doesn't and shouldn't move any part of his body, B will be able to detect that A has stopped condensing his one point. The eyelashes or cheeks will begin to move a little or a dark shadow will be cast across his face. Each person has his own way of expressing this but it is always discernible. At that instant B will be able to push A over by the shoulder,(*fig. 10*).

In conclusion the one point in the lower abdomen is not a tangible point but a point infinitely condensed. The one point in the lower abdomen is important but don't stop your mind there. While condensing to infinite smallness, if it becomes too small to perceive, just leave it as it is. *Ki* is the infinite gathering of infinitely small particles. When the mind is refined to this degree, for the first time one can become one with the universal.

Once you understand that you have the center of the universe in your abdomen, try to begin every action from this point and absorb everything and every influence into this point. Then you will be able to keep coordination of mind and body in your daily life.

FOUR BASIC PRINCIPLES TO UNIFY MIND AND BODY

a couple of sorry people

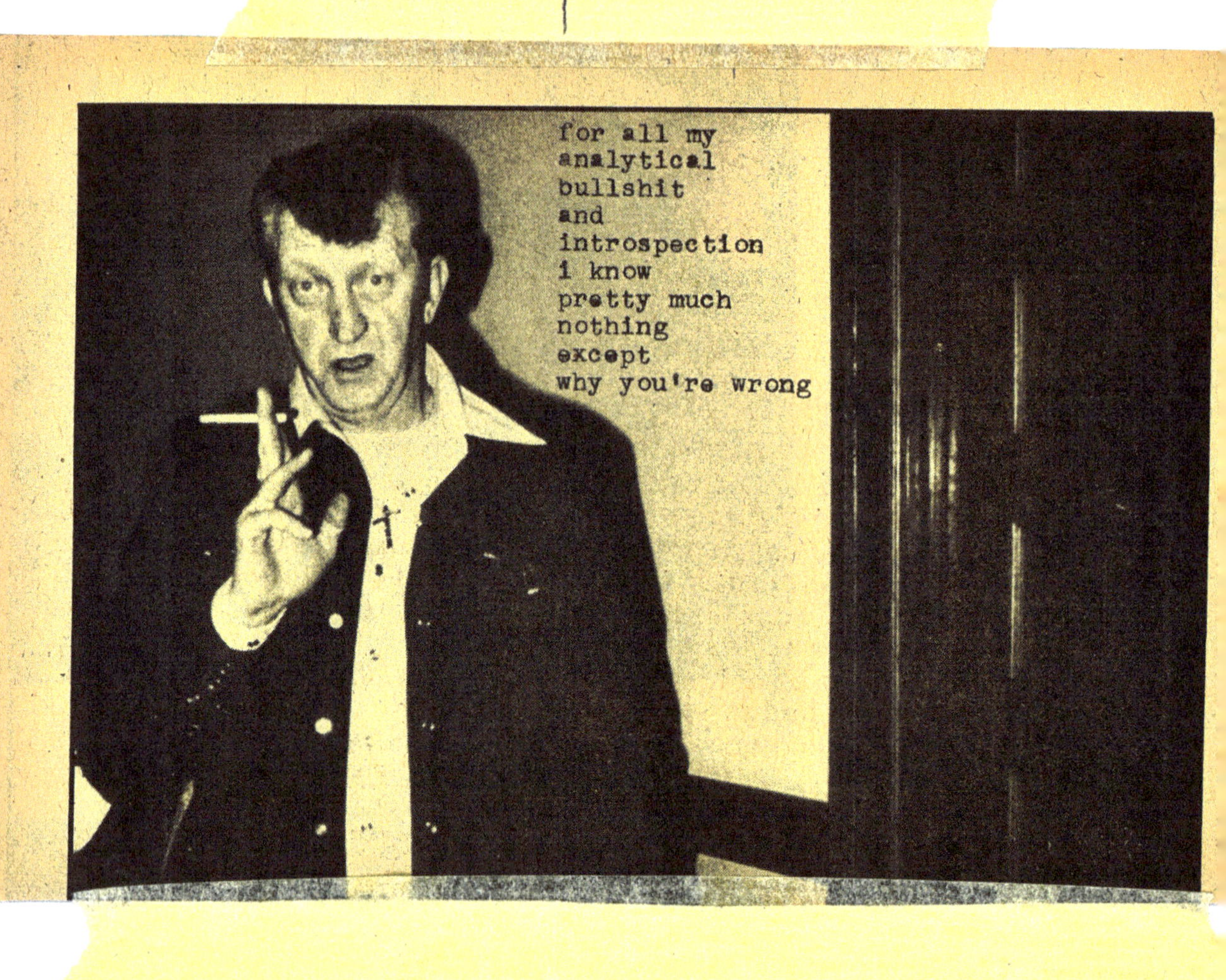

a grower and a shower

e hea

the head and the heart
neitherr very smart
both mistakenly
think the other
is the dumb one

4/2/21

~~the head and the heart~~
~~both think the other~~
~~is dümb~~
~~though neither is smart~~

the head and the heart
neith r very smart

~~think the other~~
~~is much dumb er~~

~~think the other~~
is

think the
other is
much dumber

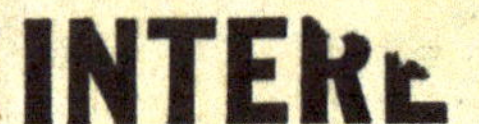

"if you wanted
to be there
they wouldn't pay you.
you aren't lucky
enough
to get paid
to do what
you want."

-dad

New developmen
tion-Electronics
expansion in Ra
create a fast g
skilled technicia
NRI home study
the lives of these
thousands of othe
page and read ho
the same path to

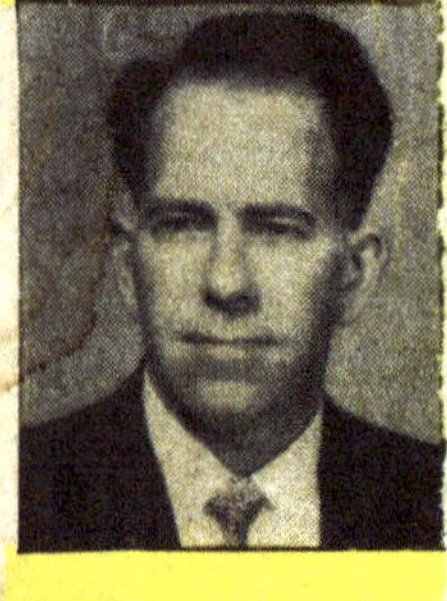

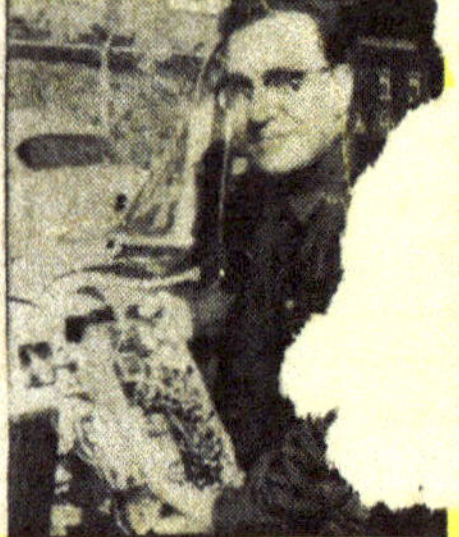

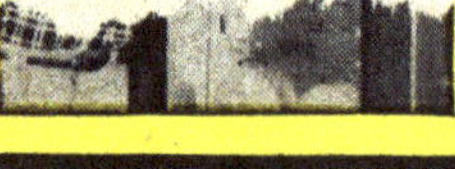

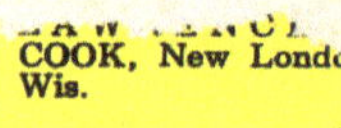

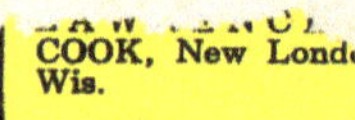

Louis, Mo.

COOK, New London, Wis.

ssile Officer
as ICBM Si
re time can
y in the po
ough I have a
job, I still
to fix radio
sets. Let the
sit back
his TV set
d my time re
it and yie
t." ALLAN
WNSEND,
, Kan.

Service Bus
of His Own
went into bu
months aft
ished the
se. It make
ly of six a
g. We repai
or radio. I
take anythin
raining with
nk it is the fi
N HOUSE,
, Texas

Microwave R
s arch at Stanf
"My first introdu
to Electronics wa
NRI Servicing co
I have had addit
training, but NRI
the groundwork f
y accomplishm
My NRI diploma
me my first jo
Electronics."
GEORGE JACKS
Menlo Park, Calif

SEE OTHER SIDE

FIRST CLASS
PERMIT
NO. 20-R
(Sec. 34.9, P.L.&R.)
Washington, D.C.

BUSINESS REPLY MAIL
NO POSTAGE STAMP NECESSARY IF MAILED IN THE UNITED STATES

POSTAGE WILL BE PAID BY

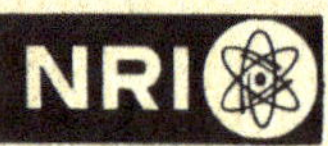

3939 Wisconsin Avenue
Washington 16, D.C.

Mail Card for Book of Facts

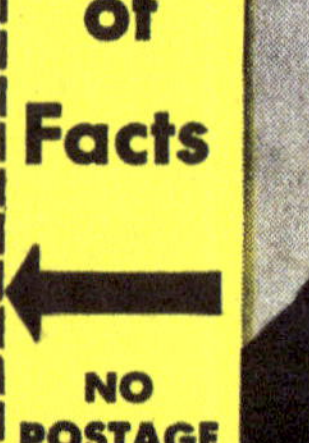

NO POSTAGE NEEDED

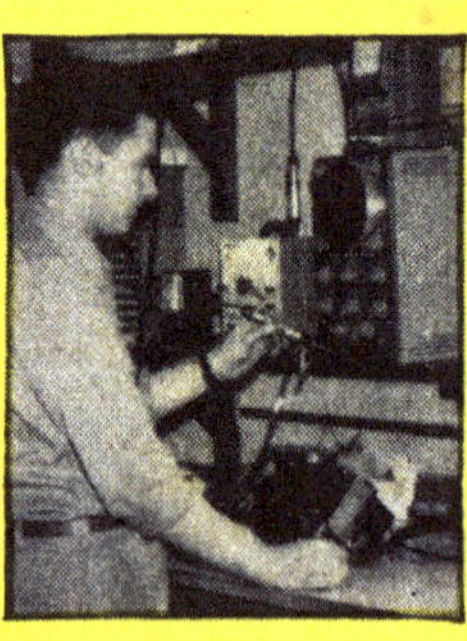

Chief Technicia
Uranium Min
"I have gone a
ever since I enr
My income at
beginning was $
month. Today I
$8,000 a year.
NRI diploma got
part-time job, to
TV engineer, bri
in another $1,
W. GERALD
LIES, Elliot
Canada

Electronic Tech
cian for Post Of
"NRI training ena
me to land a very
job as Electronic T
nician with the
Office Dept. I fin
6th out of 139. I
have a very profi
spare-time busine
ing radios and
NORMAN R.
STON, Cincinn
Ohio.

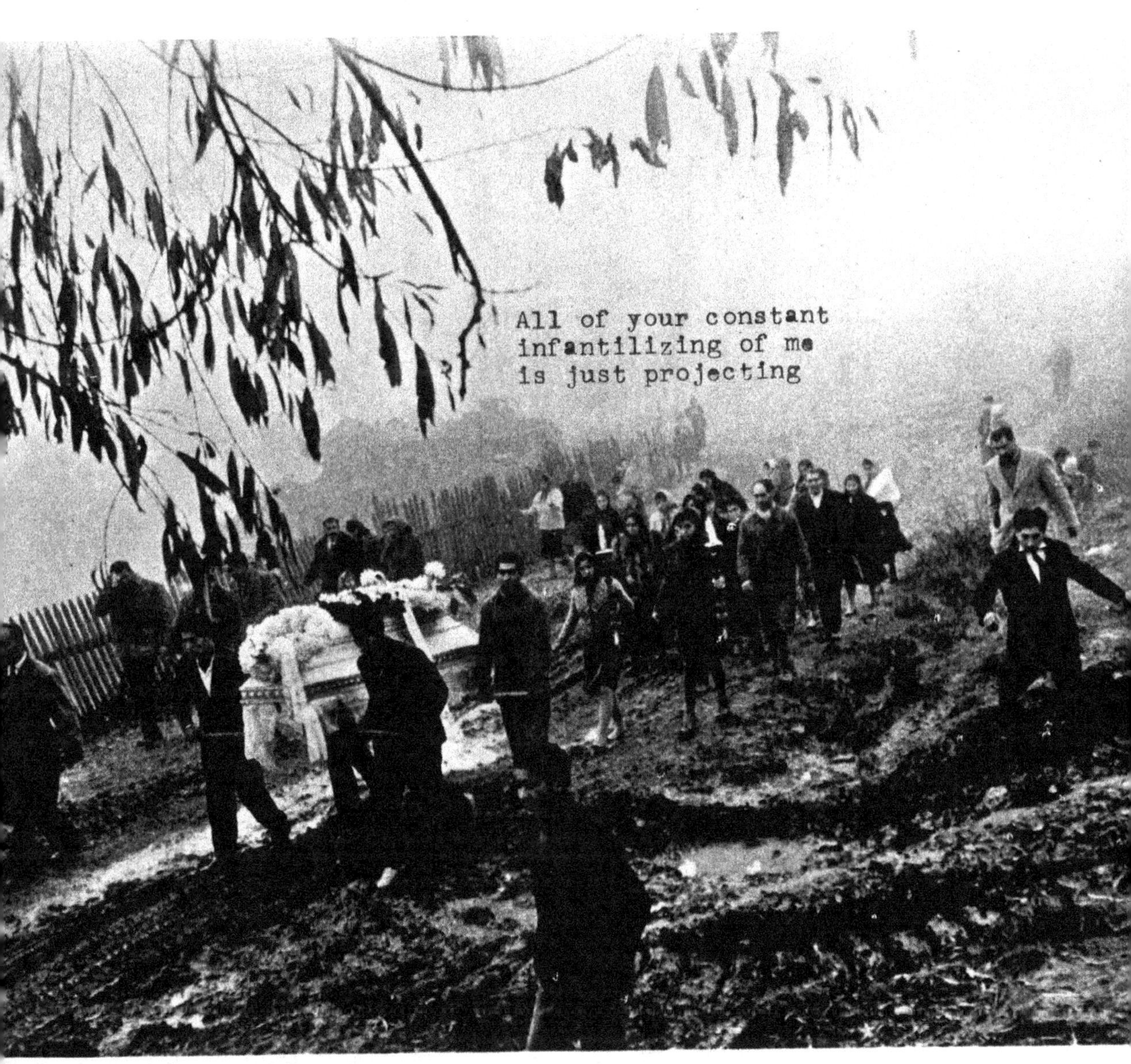

Jarabina, 1963

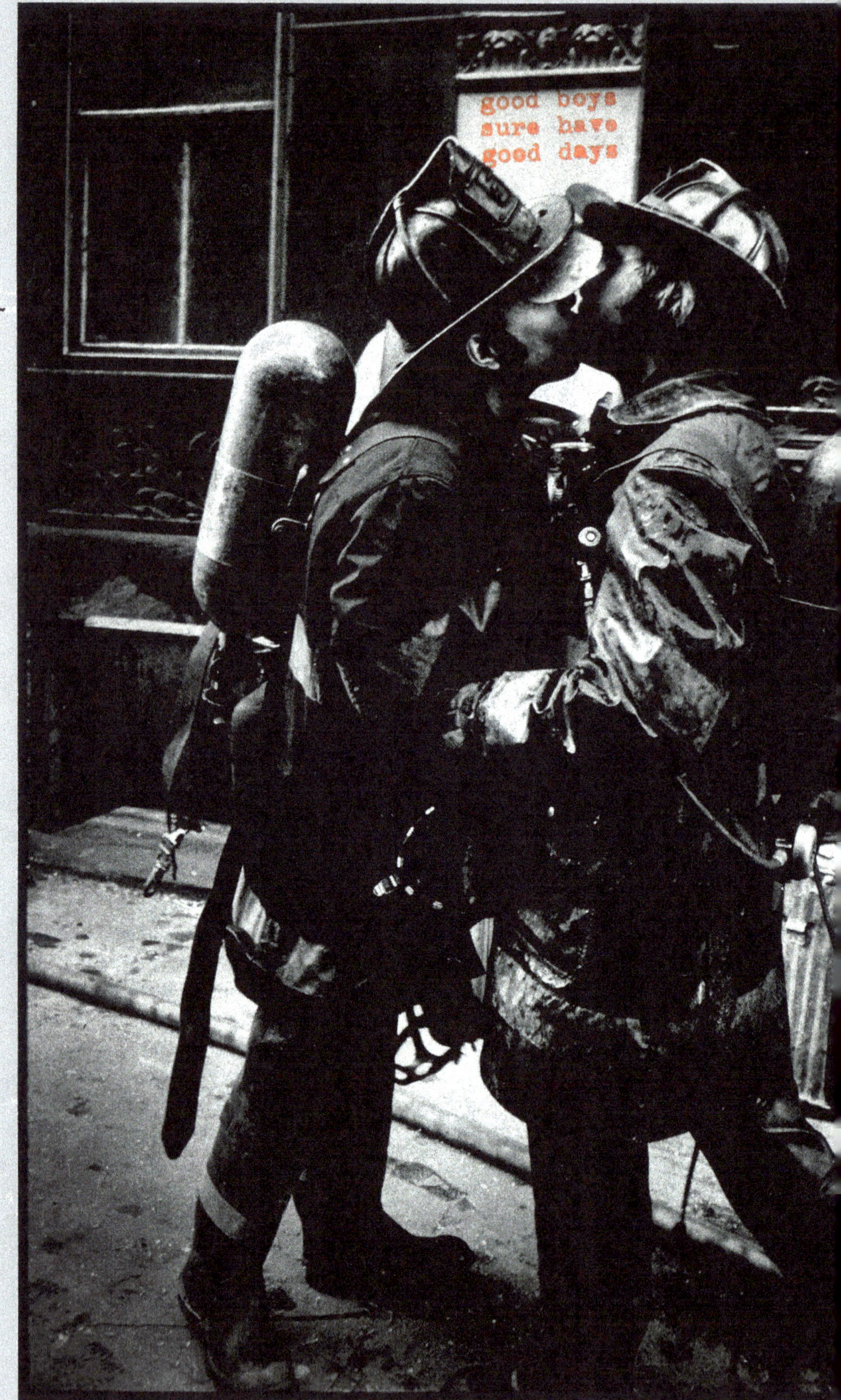

*surviving another apartment-house
een carrying oxygen tanks share the
embracing. "It's not unusual to see
ugging, kissing," observes fireman-
h. The embraces, he says, convey a
all right, if you need me, I'll be there."*

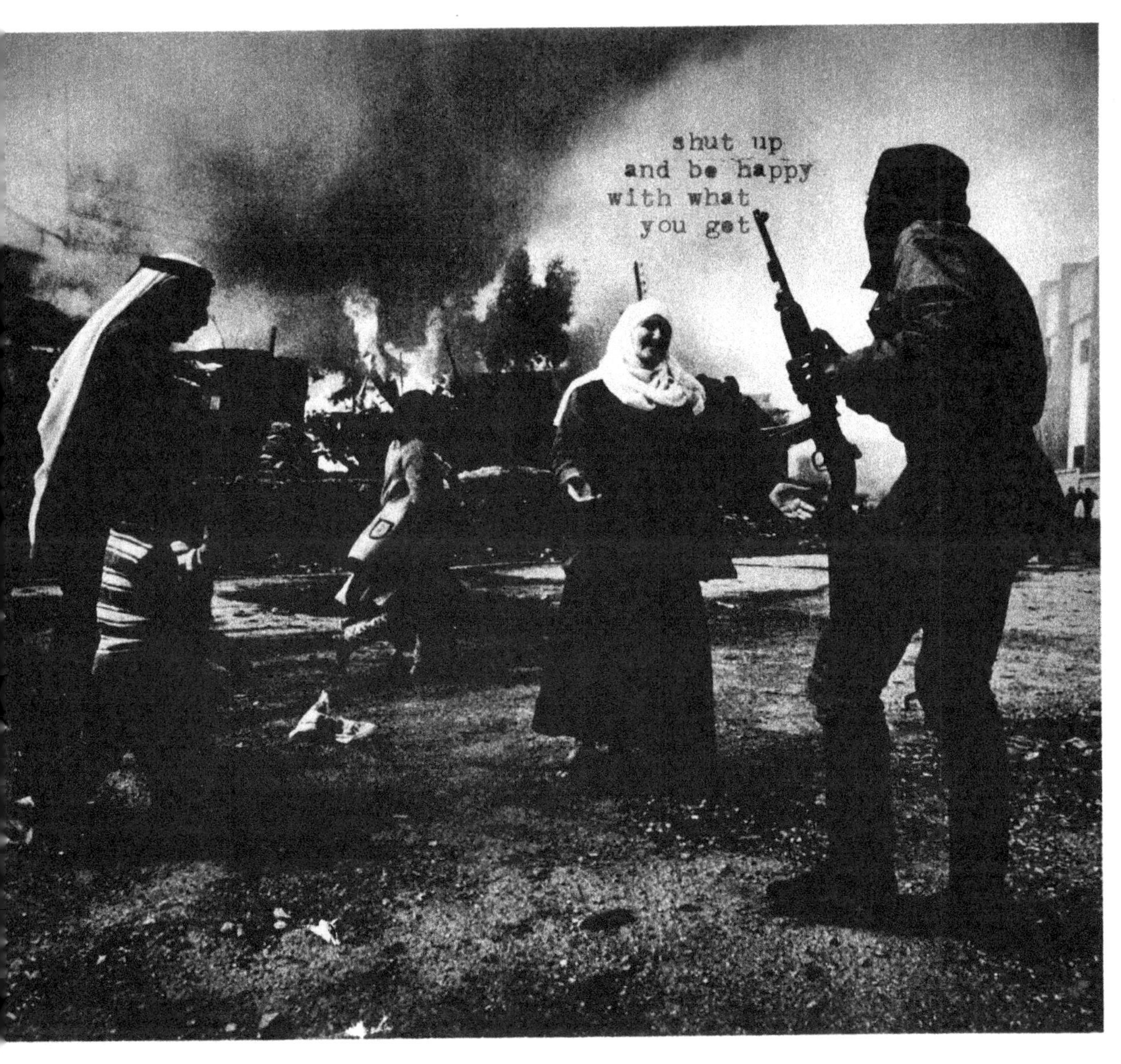
shut up
and be happy
with what
you get

July 4th 2021

i hope everyone
had fun
complaining
today.

3.63

3.64 DANIEL HUNTINGTON (1816–1906)
Skeleton Study (ca. 1848)
Charcoal, crayon, and white chalk. 15⅛ × 9⅞ in.
Brooklyn Museum of Art. Gift of Roebling Society.
68.167.3.

Down

The following exercises suggest some ways of studying the skeleton. When necessary, they may be simplified to suit your drawing skills. Some of these exercises may suggest other ways of learning to understand the skeleton's forms and proportions and to stimulate your interest in its creative possibilities. Do not hesitate to explore any approach to familiarizing yourself with the skeleton. The only wrong way to regard the skeleton is with a casual eye, born of the misconception that what is not actually visible on the figure's surface is less important than what can be seen by the naked eye.

In doing these exercises, use any erasable medium and any compatible drawing surface. Although none of these exercises is restricted by time, none can be usefully experienced in fewer than forty-five minutes; some may take you considerably longer. Because your aim is to familiarize yourself with skeletal facts, you may wish to develop these exercises in several drafts on tracing paper. By placing a first draft under a fresh sheet of tracing paper, you can quickly redraw it, making corrections more easily than by extensive erasures on the same sheet. Furthermore, reversing the tracing paper to examine the drawing helps you quickly see errors in scale, shape, structure, and location.

1. Referring to a skeleton, anatomy texts, or the illustrations in this chapter, draw two detailed studies of the skeleton as it would appear from the poses shown in Figures 3.65 and 3.66. Your drawing should approach the degree of precision in Figure 3.66.

2. Rework or redraw several of your figure drawings (or draw any of the photos of the figure in this book), thinning down the forms to exaggerate the skeleton's influence on the surface forms. The results should suggest emaciated figures, as in Figure 3.60.

3. Using the skeleton or any other visual reference material to assist you, make a *simplified* drawing of either a

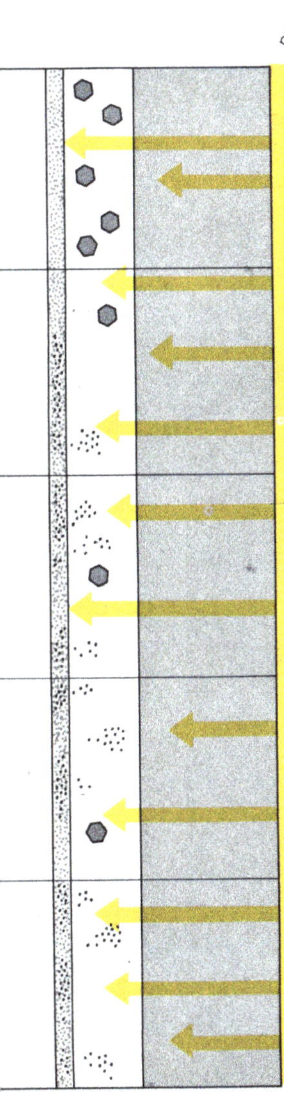

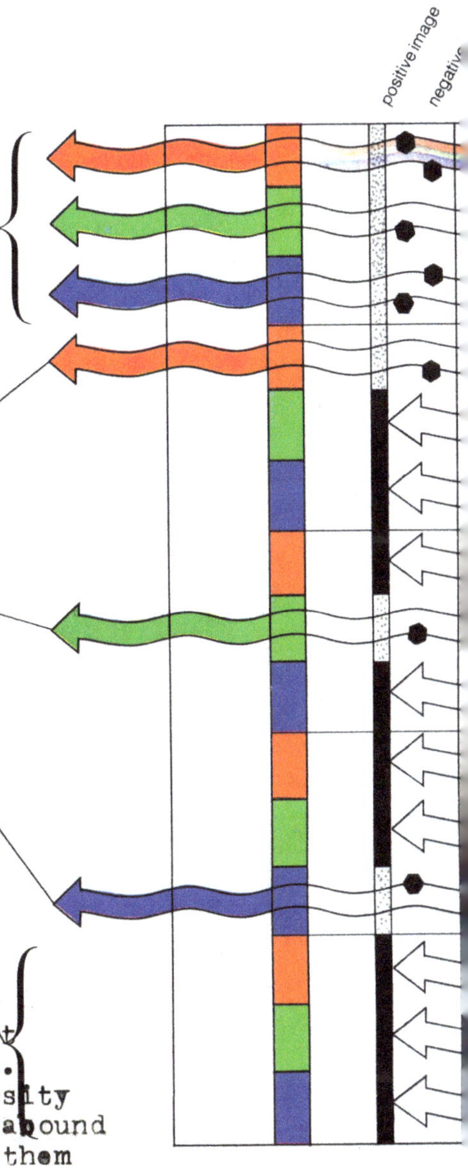

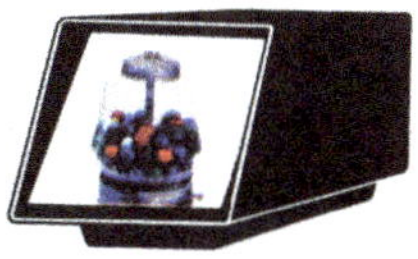

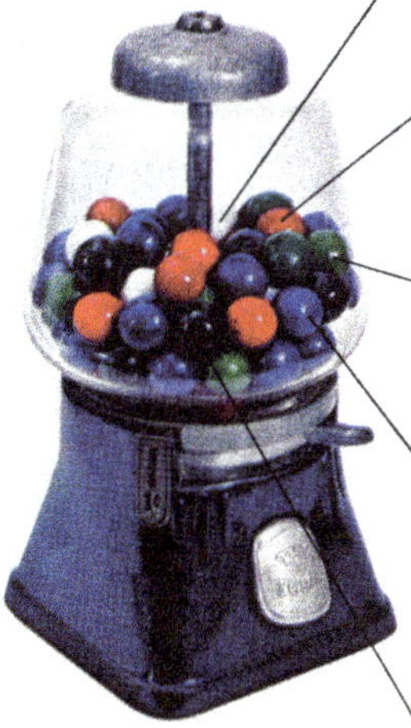

It's the people who pretend
they don't pay attention
who seem to know the most
about what I'm doin.
What made you all this way?
This is no creativity desert
rather, an oasis of outlets.
I see no champions of adversity
but lazies and do-nothings abound
the hard working few among them
maintaining the system.
such fragility
unable to appreciate things
outside of what can be touched.
A caustic culture of socialites
with no sociability
morally bankrupt
self proclaimed truth seekers
incapable of honesty
and I guess I'd better stop
before I get to myself

ocessing fluid (yellow line and ove) penetrates three layers o' half a second. It bleaches away the ray tones) and develops the the emulsion layer to form the silver gons) that make up the negative usly, the processing fluid dissolves stals (black dots), which then ving layer. There the dissolved silver around chemical particles (gray hin patches of metallic silver that e image. Stabilizers from the enetrate the other layers to protect r from chemical residues.

For viewing, white light from a bulb insid goes through the now-transparent ant only slightly obstructed by the widely grains of the negative image in the en the receiving layer, the silver patches positive stop all light except that need picture. The positive image of the red light before it reaches the green and stripes but admits it to the red stripe, light goes through the filter to the view The images of the green and blue bal that of the white ball lets light through three colors, which are recombined b white light. The black ball's image kee

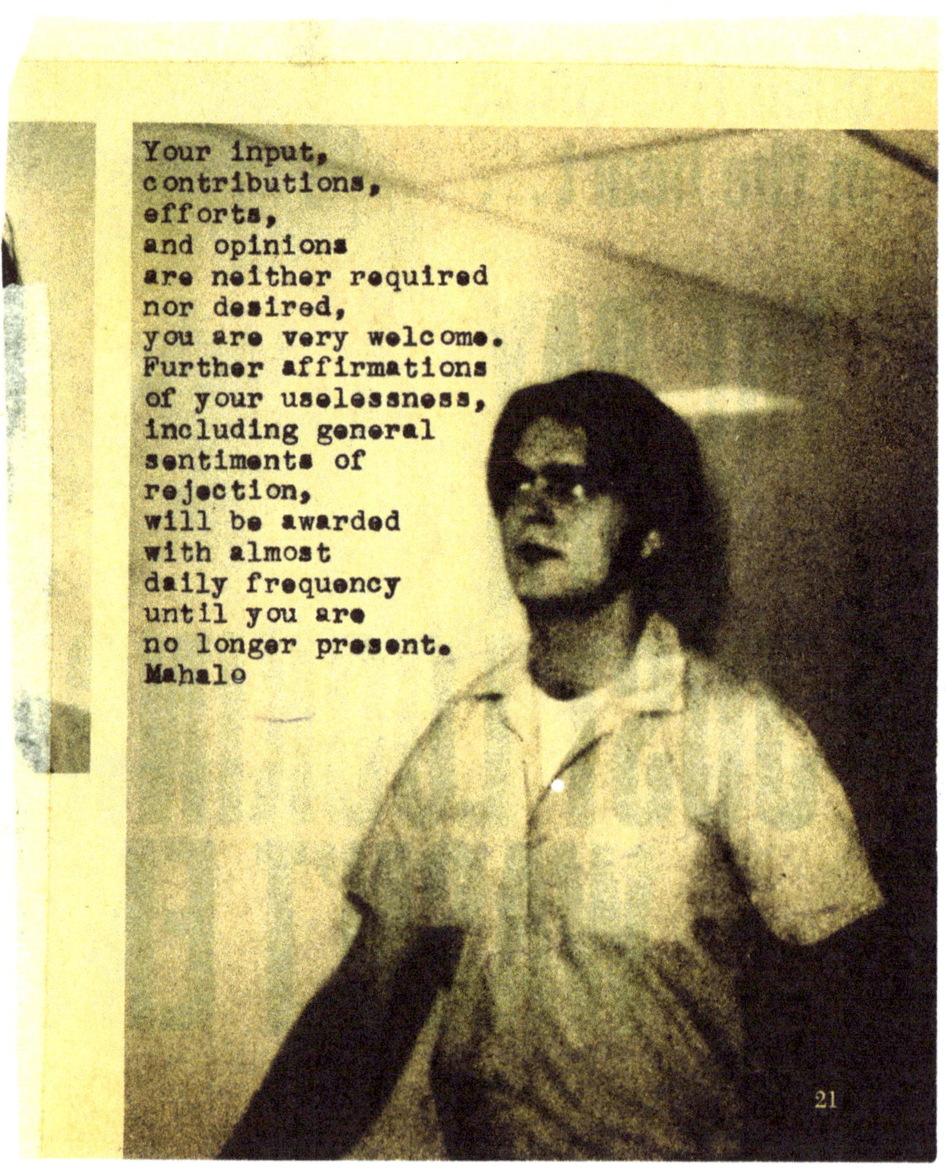
Your input,
contributions,
efforts,
and opinions
are neither required
nor desired,
you are very welcome.
Further affirmations
of your uselessness,
including general
sentiments of
rejection,
will be awarded
with almost
daily frequency
until you are
no longer present.
Mahalo
21

No thanks

After much deliberation,
and in light of the last
300,000 years or so,
I have decided that I will no longer
be involving myself with
The Human Race.
In my 32 years of participation
they have proven themselves
to be a rather unsavory group
and I feel I can no longer associate
myself or my image
with such a problematic,
and toxic,
and generally unkind
kind.
Thank you for your continued support.
Mahalo

NAFU THAT'S

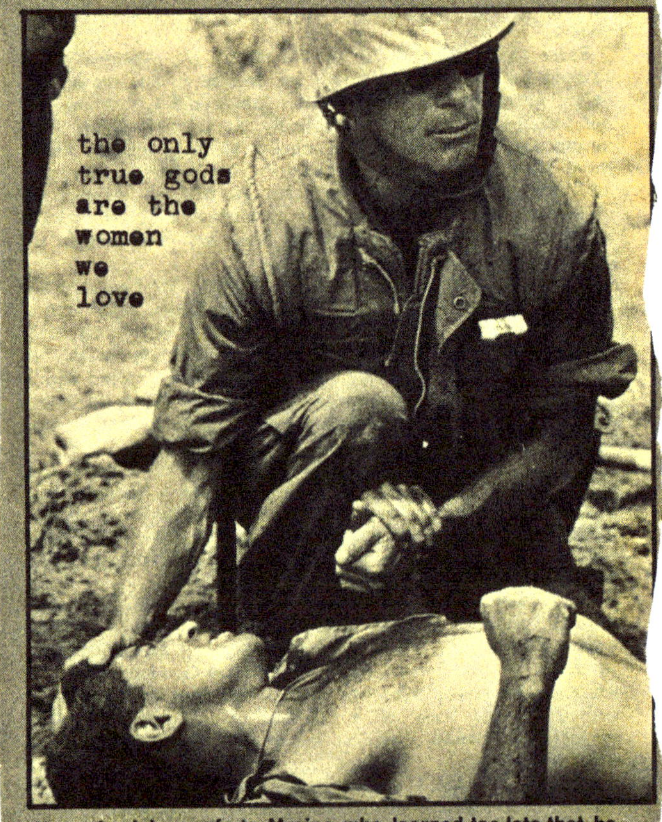

Navy chaplain comforts Marine who learned too late that he held inferior rifle when he contacted VC at Quang Tri City. Scandal has rocked Pentagon, but the slaughter still goes on.

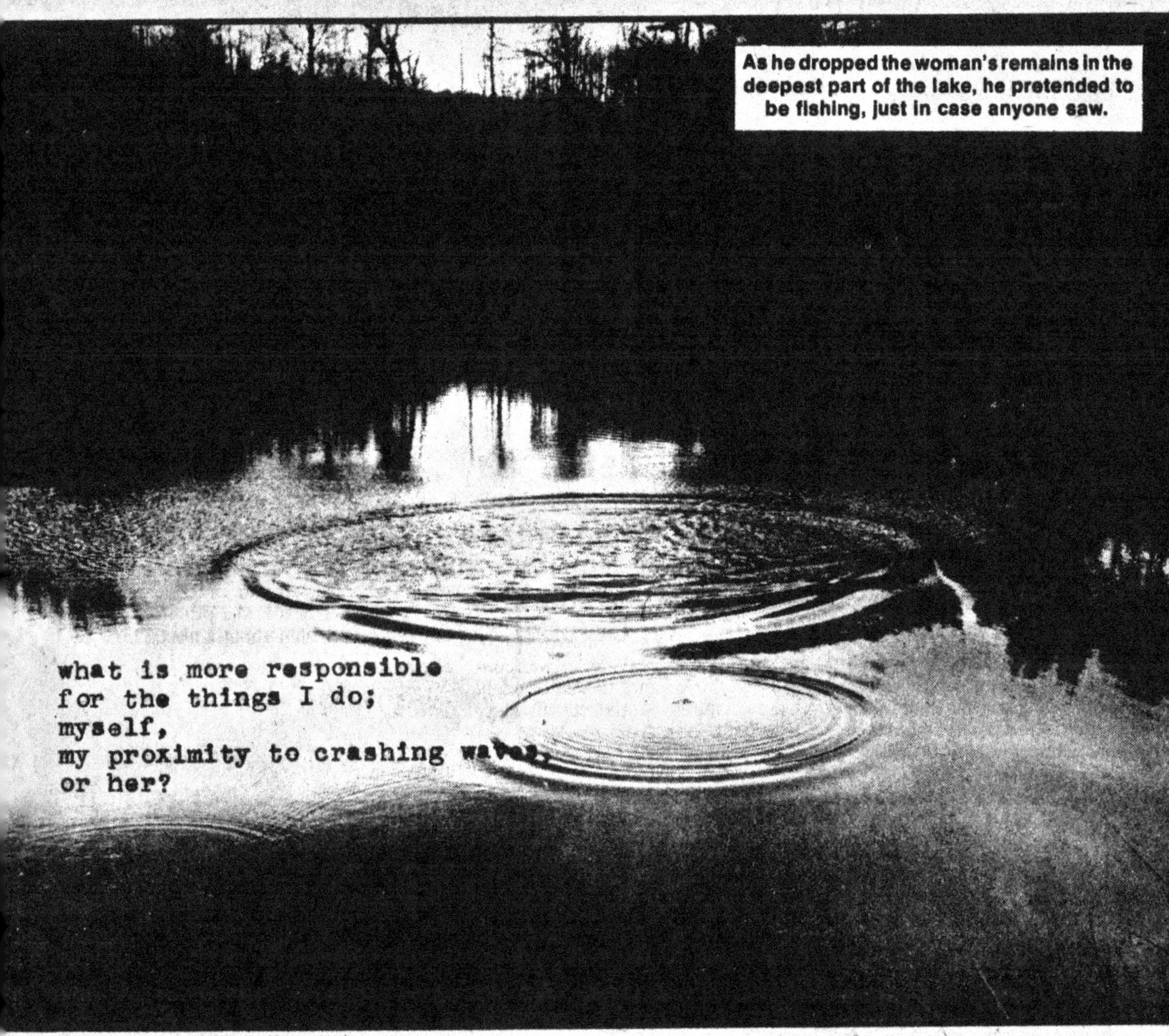

As he dropped the woman's remains in the deepest part of the lake, he pretended to be fishing, just in case anyone saw.

He came in straight from the field, wearing faded blue jeans and a Navy blue T-shirt bearing the lettering, "Underwater School of America." As he sat nervously down in a chair in the downtown Minneapolis office, the deputies read him his rights under the Miranda decision, and asked, "Do you want a lawyer."

Looking directly at his questioners, Dave Hoffman declared, "God will be my lawyer."

He then told the deputies a story that made their blood run cold.

After weeks of abstinence from sex, Hoffman said he made amorous advances toward his wife on Saturday night — the night before she disappeared — and she turned to him and said, "Why don't you go downstairs and sleep with your mom?"

He loved Carol, he told the deputies, but he decided then and there that he would have to "get rid of the evil in my house." On Sunday, August 10, he said, "I told my mom I was going to have to put her (Carol) to sleep. Tonight's got to be the night."

He said his mother responded, "It will be for the best," or, "It would be the best for the kids."

That night, he said, Carol tantalized him by coming to bed naked. Once again he began to make sexual advances, but Carol turned her back on him. Nevertheless, Hoffman said, he kissed Carol and caressed her, and shifted his body on top of hers.

Then he put his hands around her throat and strangled her as she uttered the last word she would ever say, "Dave!"

"I kept squeezing tighter and tighter and tighter... until she went limp," Hoffman told the stunned deputies. "When my arms got tired, I placed my knees around her neck and squeezed again. I was removing the evil from my house. You do believe in God, don't yo

"Dave, what happened to Carol did you do with her body?"

"I took her into the bathroom," lained nervously. "Then I went d the basement and awakened my m told her I needed her to stand gua side the bathroom door, so wouldn't come in, in case she w during the night."

Hoffman said his 65-year-old put on her robe, came upstair stretched out on a couch oppos bathroom door. He then went i bathroom, closed the door, an ceeded to dismember Carol Lynn bathtub of her dream house.

But first, he told the deputies, scissors and clipped his wife's hair he later burned in a wood stove.

Then, with a 10-inch serrated

miss you

What ghosts am I not finding?
I'd love to find one

I'd like to talk I mean

What ghosts am I not finding?
There's one I'd
love to see
but we don't talk much ever
cause I don't know
where I'm not lookin

In that place
where that ghost is

I desperately long to be

there's something
you will discover
about openness in
honest efforts to
define emptiness.

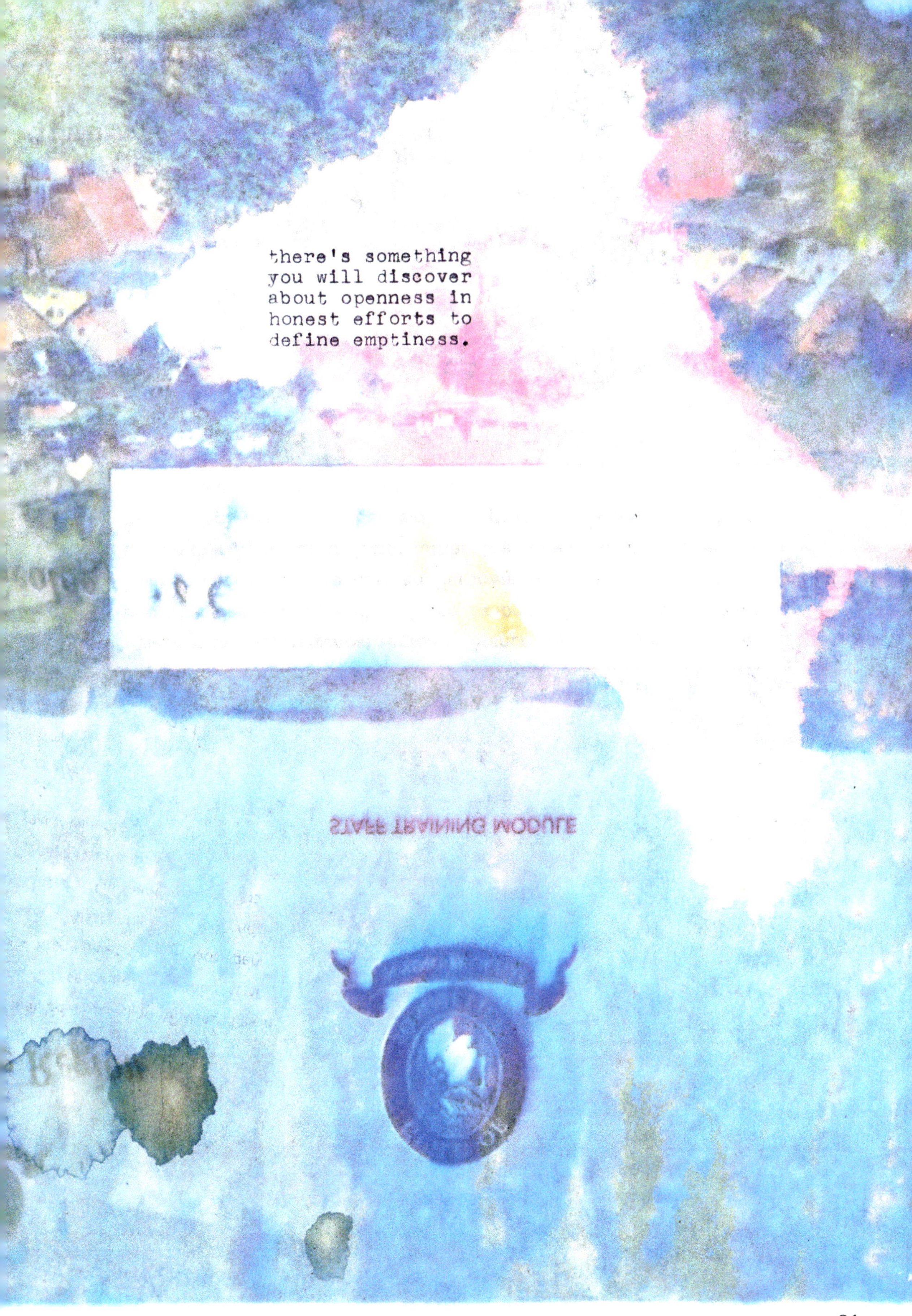

GO TO BED

there's a chance I don't wake up tomorrow
there's a chance I don't wake up tomorrow
If I don't
know that I resented all of it.
and everything I tried to be
for all of you
I lived with far more intention
than anyone ever
gave me credit for
I left this place
loving
far more than I was ever loved
and I hope you carry that with you
And I hope it makes you better
than the version of you
I loved
before I left

bated breath

I am still
I'm all the movement
you can find
in something perfectly still.
with bated breath and
lungs to fill
I'll suffocate
before I move . . . .

I am still
I'm all the movement
you can find
in something perfectly still.

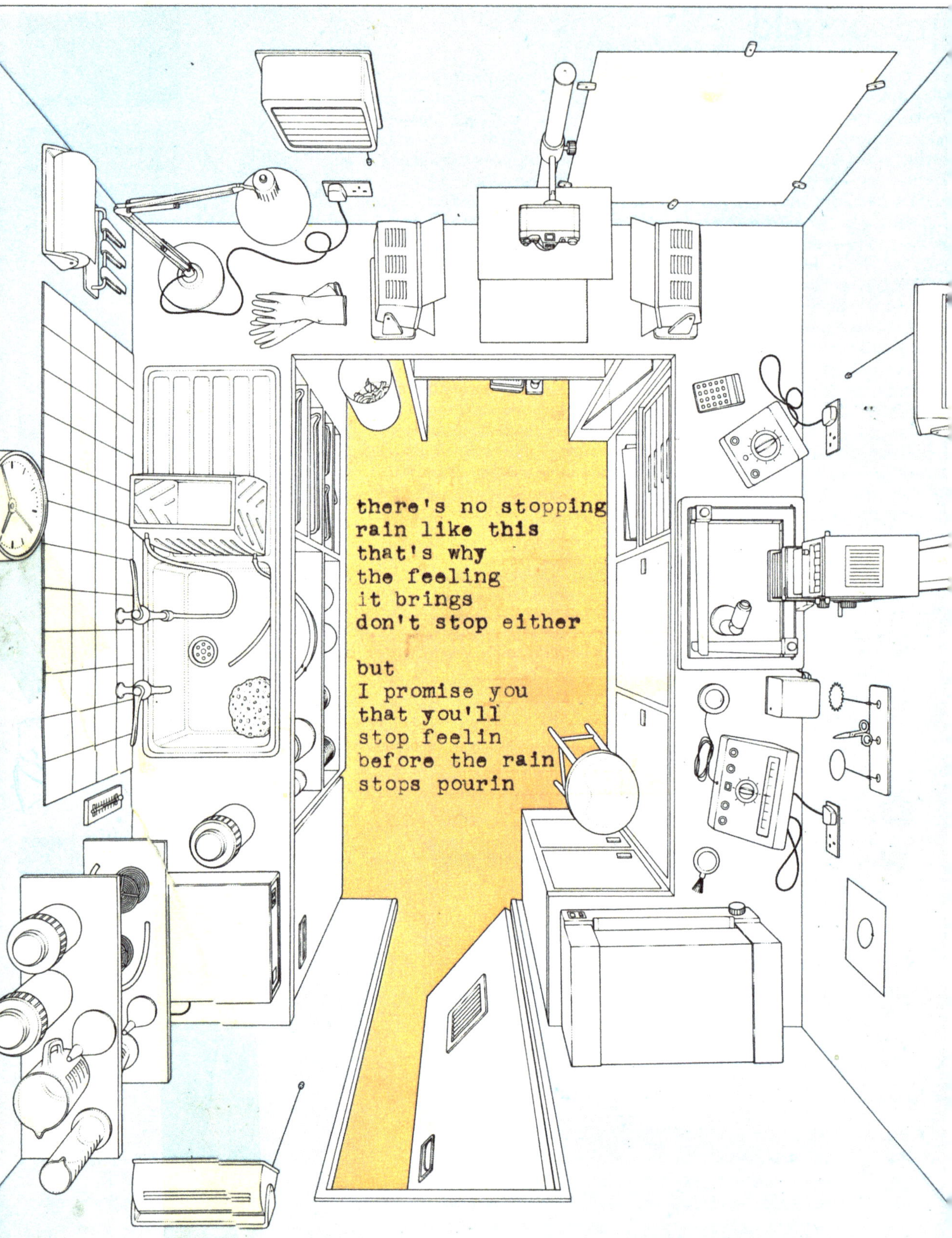

there's no stopping
rain like this
that's why
the feeling
it brings
don't stop either

but
I promise you
that you'll
stop feelin
before the rain
stops pourin

Zack

I remember this one Halloween
Zack had finally confronted
that bully he'd had
Ron, I think, was his name
and anyway he'd beaten him
not like men beat each other
but the red-faced embarassing way
that boys do.
Beat him as soon as he'd seen him
walking along the sidewalk of the main street
in the dark but early evening
on that last day
in small town Kansas October.
Just hit him a whole bunch and all at once
and Ron wasn't ready at all.
We all were so happy and proud of him
there and I remember it
in moments the rain stops
and the air is cool and still
on cloudy February nights
in Honolulu's chinatown.
Somehow I'm there again in my head
and I remember too
it had something to do
with some girl.
Something with an "S" maybe
I forget her name
who cares?
Zack's dead now
He's been dead for some time
He shot himself in the head
I still don't remember what's-her-face.

Chris

I wish Chris didn't grow up so poor
with all the problems that come with that.
and I wish the whole thing
had been easier for him.
I think about this one time
his dad had been drinking and had caught
a turtle and grilled it
and I remember trying some of it
with Chris and he'd said he eats turtle
all the time.
I don't remember it tasting all that bad.
I wish the frustration of poverty
hadn't driven him into drugs and crime
the way it did.
and I wish he wasn't schizophrenic
and I wish he would take his meds.
I wish his parents weren't there
when he shot himself today
in the house he grew up in
across the street from my childhood home.
I wish things had been different for Chris.

only if it's gluten free

There was a guy once
and this guy pounded
rice and wheat
and whatever
into flour.
And this poor bastard pounded this shit
into flour
and made something new.
The world he knew was taken by it
and men who knew him
did it and taught their sons to do it
and those sons taught their sons
to do all this fice or wheat or whatever pounding
and lots of sons of sons
did plenty pounding of shit into flour
and paying for whores.
There was bread and cakes and crackers
and whores got plenty of it.
One day some son had enough
and figured he ought to matter more
than all the happy bread-fed whores
and whote down how to do the pounding
he figured out how to live forever
and now sons who've never met him
read what he wrote when writing was new
and still make plenty
bread for whores

maximum effort

well...
I'm here, now
in the middle of february
and I guess
there's always tomorrow

"there's always tomorrow"
has never resulted in chills
it has never made a man die for anything
and never made a man think about doing any dying

"there's always tomorrow"
has never preceded an existential crisis
it has never made a man stray from sleep
and never made a man think sleep would kill him

"there's always tomorrow"
has never kept a man from death
it has never made a man do any honest loving
and never made aman think honestly of love

I've wasted a whole year
and nearly two months now
tryin to talk
it's fuckin february
what a waste

alone time

I went
to that beach
to be alone
and to know it
while I was there.
I just laid out though
and thought about that
and you too.
I'm done thinking about you.
You can't even give me
any freedom
alone at the beach.

My, oh my
what tides you bring in
without even trying.
You night lighting moon.
Illuminating all this darkness.
You cosmic beauty.
I just spend my nights
looking up at you.
I spend my days
on the beach
interrupted by your tide.

I sold drugs to feed myself
I done worse than that
I did nasty shit to stick around
still i was wrongfully evicted
during a pandemic
during a global economic collapse
cause they knew i couldn't fight it
but i kept working
six days a week
no overtime
head down
to keep my job and not be fired
to solidify my place
in an extremely nepotistic
unwelcoming environment
where all of the people like you
knew without a worry
you'd just walk back in
wiped my ass with napkins
from fast food joints
made new soles for worn through shoes
with stolen duct tape
cooked for friends
that could pay for the food
and you
you lent me money
i guess there's that
money i paid in taxes
money the government then gave you
money you didn't need
money you didn't earn
and you badmouthed me
to all my "friends"
and treated me like i was less than you
and i paid your bitch ass back
and then some
and i'm the piece of shit
you fuck
put your hands in front of your face
next time you see me
from now on
you'll be badmouthing me
with no fuckin teeth

THORAX **from the right side**

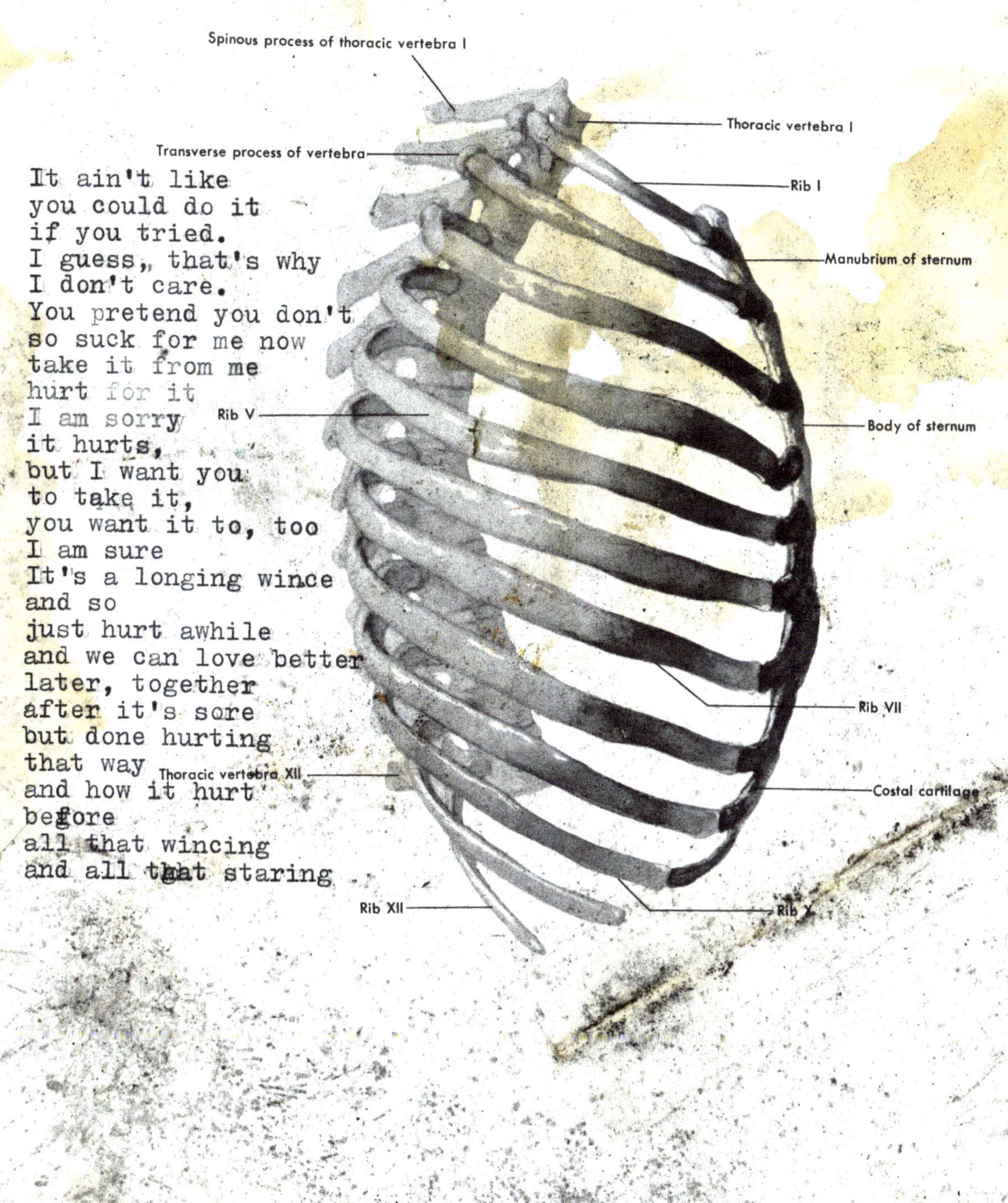

It ain't like
you could do it
if you tried.
I guess, that's why
I don't care.
You pretend you don't
so suck for me now
take it from me
hurt for it
I am sorry
it hurts,
but I want you
to take it,
you want it to, too
I am sure
It's a longing wince
and so
just hurt awhile
and we can love better
later, together
after it's sore
but done hurting
that way
and how it hurt
before
all that wincing
and all that staring

washed ashore

my sleep
is always deep
i never hear
anything
but, a woman's bare feet on tile floor
the lethargic cadence
a soft warm slap
against the smooth
pre-dawn cold
erotic lazy lapping of small waves
moving around me and about
i can hear
that

it erodes me to nothing
waves make sand of earth

getting tired of these

when I leave this here
once I'm done with it.
then I leave it behind
I don't write anything
I can't think anything

who is ready for pain?
who moves forward with
turmoil, anguish, hurt
that moves without you
saying it's own thing?

which one of you is it
that's brave enough to
exist where the truths
finally concede to you
that you're the victor

who's ready to try the
things I did, but win?
who's ready to triumph
over the limitations I
struggled to beat just
to give you what I am?

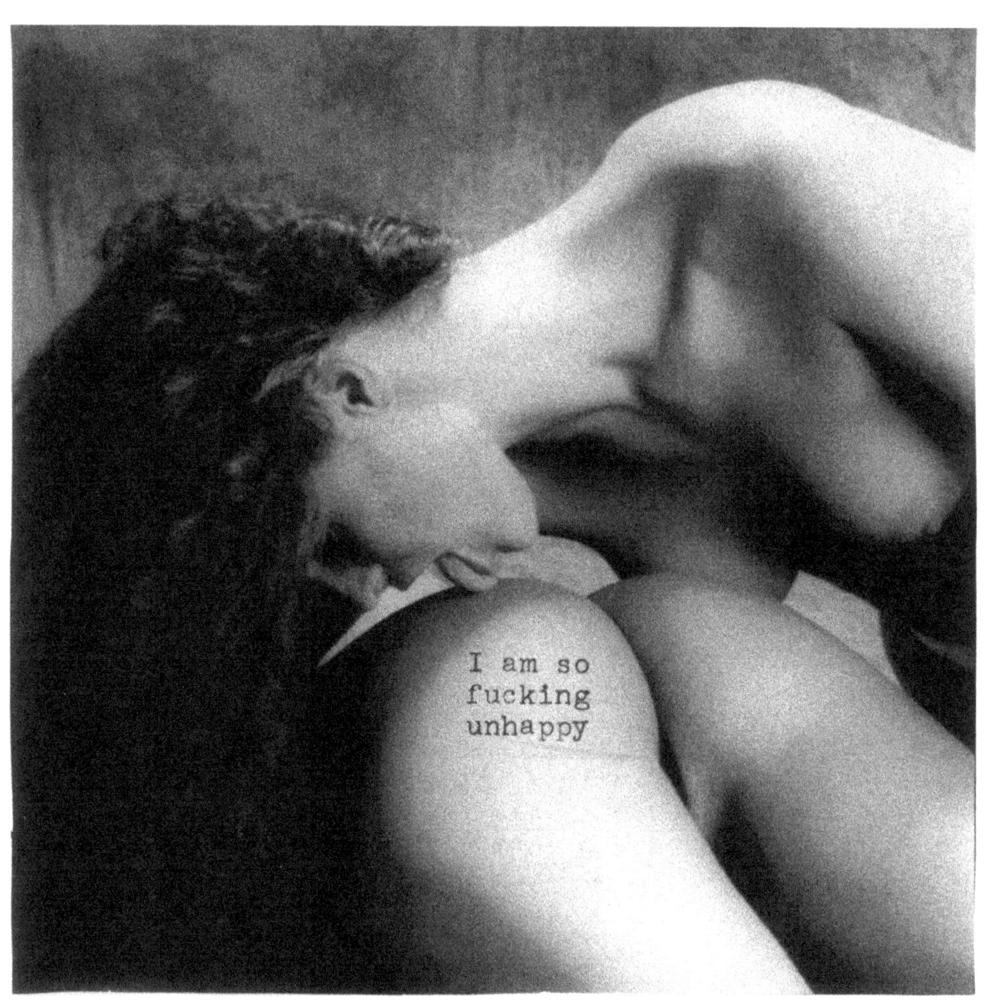
I am so
fucking
unhappy

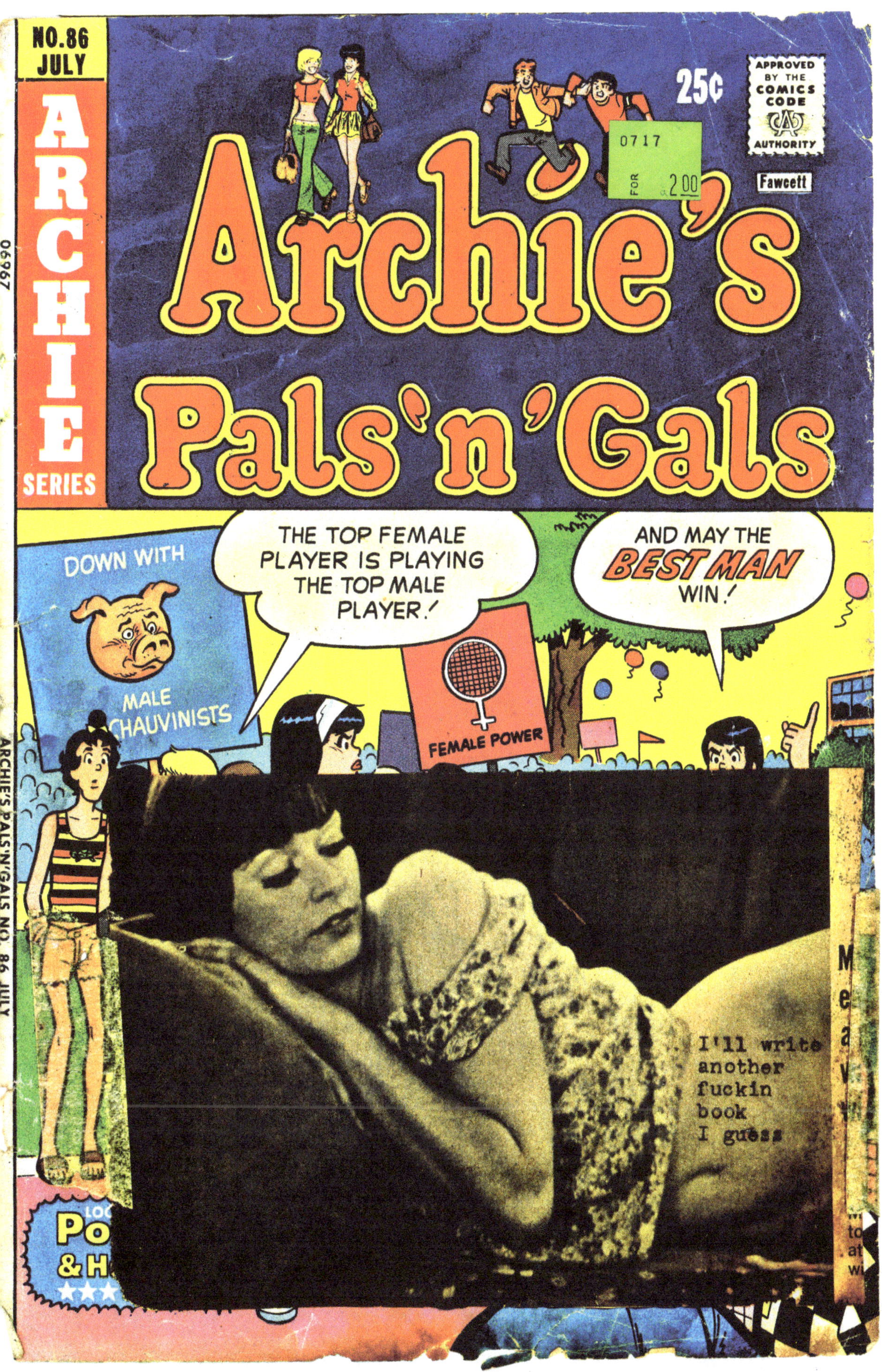

NO.86
JULY
ARCHIE
SERIES
25¢
APPROVED BY THE COMICS CODE AUTHORITY
Fawcett
Archie's
Pals'n'Gals
DOWN WITH
MALE CHAUVINISTS
THE TOP FEMALE PLAYER IS PLAYING THE TOP MALE PLAYER!
AND MAY THE BEST MAN WIN!
FEMALE POWER
ARCHIE'S PALS'N'GALS NO. 86 JULY
I'll write
another
fuckin
book
I guess

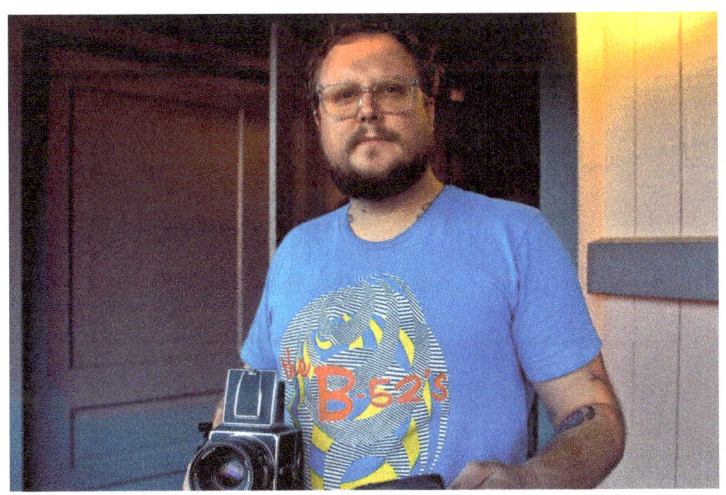

Tony Kile is originally from Kansas City, but left in a hurry at 18. He is a submarine veteran and now works in food and beverage. He is starting to collect art. The man's been eating real good and it shows; he's a little overweight at the moment but he's working on it. Kile will be writing longer things soon. He currently resides in Honolulu. He has two orange cats.

www.ingramcontent.com/pod-product-compliance
Lightning Source LLC
LaVergne TN
LVHW080332110826
845155LV00024B/151

* 9 7 8 1 9 4 4 5 2 1 2 5 7 *